NOSTALG
DARLINGTON

TRUE NORTH BOOKS

DEAN CLOUGH

HALIFAX

WEST YORKSHIRE

HX3 5AX

TEL 01422 344344

THE PUBLISHERS WOULD LIKE TO THANK THE FOLLOWING COMPANIES FOR SUPPORTING THE PRODUCTION OF THIS BOOK

MAIN SPONSOR
AMDEGA LIMITED

ERNEST BENNETT & CO. (DARLINGTON) LIMITED

BURTS CARPETS

BUSSEY & ARMSTRONG LIMITED

PATONS & BALDWINS LIMITED

THE CORNMILL SHOPPING CENTRE

JC & NH MURRAY LIMITED

REXAM CORRUGATED NORTH EAST LIMITED

SANDERSON FORD (DARLINGTON) LIMITED

SEATON LENG & SON LIMITED

SHEPHERD & COMPANY (DARLINGTON) LIMITED

H TAYLOR & SONS

KEN WARNE LIMITED

THOMAS WATSON & SON

First published in Great Britain by True North Books
Dean Clough
Halifax HX3 5AX
1997

ISBN 1 900 463 31 8

Introduction

Welcome to *Nostalgic Darlington,* a look back on the town through a series of lovely old photographs, chosen according to their ability to rekindle memories of the past. A period which is generally within the experience of many readers has been chosen, the aim being to stimulate memories of life and events in the area. This means that the emphasis is firmly upon events and scenes we can remember - this is not a book about bowler-hats and crinolines! Neither is *Nostalgic Darlington* a work of 'local history' in the normal sense of the word; it has far more to do with entertainment than serious study, but we hope you will agree that it is none the worse for that. It is hoped that the images on the following pages will prompt memories of the Darlington known by readers in times gone by; we are always pleased to receive letters from people who can add to the information provided, so that we can enhance future reprints of our books. Many local companies and organisations have allowed us to study their archives to recount their history on these pages - and fascinating reading it makes too for anyone interested in the development of these well-known local businesses. The present-day guardians of the companies concerned are proud of their products and the achievements of their people. We are pleased to play our part by making it possible for them to share their history with a wider audience.

Darlington market in the early 50s. Then, as now, a bustling centre of bargains, characters and colour.

When we began compiling *Nostalgic Darlington* several months ago we anticipated that the task would be a pleasurable one, but our expectations have been greatly surpassed. The quality of the photographs we have been privileged to use has been superb, and the assistance we have received from the staff at the *Northern Echo* and Darlington's Local Studies Library has made our work very enjoyable. There is a tremendous passion in the town about the Darlington of the past. We are pleased to have played a small part in supplying more images and information for the growing appetite among nostalgia buffs and ordinary people who are increasingly interested in times gone by.

Darlington is variously known as 'The Railway Town', 'The Quaker Town', and 'The Market Town.' We prefer to think of Darlington simply as one of the nicest all-round places in which one could hope to live, a place with a remarkable past and innovations which have influenced the world. The Darlington & Stockton Railway served to put the area on the historical map when it was built in 1825. Darlington had been involved in the production of textile goods for at least seven centuries before the railways were born, and the area became well known for the quality and ingenuity of its engineers from the turn of the nineteenth century onwards. Versatility is a word which frequently crops up when accounts are given about Darlington's industrial past. Innovation in the field of education led to the town being recognised as a pioneer in the field of nursery education.

Entertainment has played an important part in the local life. The first animated feature was shown at the Mechanic's Institute in 1897. By the late 1930s Darlington had more cinema seats per head of population than any other town in the country.

The area is lucky to be graced by the presence of some fine architecture. The spire of St. Cuthbert's Church has dominated the skyline since the 14th century. Of course, the church has been in existence since the end of the twelfth century, but the phenomenal 150 ton spire was a later addition. The market buildings and *town clock* may be taken for granted sometimes by local people who have grown up with them - but these imposing Darlington *icons* get some well-deserved coverage in the following pages. Some of our favourite pictures are those which show Darlington people celebrating, shopping, relaxing or enjoying a works party. For it is *people* who make the 'difference' in a town, and Darlington people can be proud of the difference they have made.

Nostalgic Darlington has been a pleasure to compile; we hope you enjoy reading it.
Happy memories!

Phil Holland and Mark Smith,
Publishers.

TEXT
PHIL HOLLAND
PAULINE BELL
DESIGN/PICTURE EDITING
MARK SMITH
MANDY WALKER
BUSINESS DEVELOPMENT
GARETH MARTIN

Contents

Section one   *Events*

Section two   *At your leisure*

Section three   *Around the town centre*

Section four   *At war*

Section five   *Wheels of time*

Section six   *Shopping spree*

Section seven   *At work*

Right: In the days before Darlington had a by-pass crossing the road could be quite a hazardous exercise. A policeman kitted out with white oversleeves was on hand to help in this early 1960s picture.

Events

Fancy dress was the order of the day when this picture was taken. The lady in the centre of the scene is thought to be Maud Fawbert, wife of the local legend Geordie Fawbert. Maud was born in 1899 and so was in her mid 40s when this picture was taken. Like her husband, she led a colourful, but hard life and was a regular trader on the market with her loads of fish wheeled from Bank Top station on her own cart. She can be seen here making a decent attempt at impersonating Winston Churchill as part of the victory celebrations which took place at the end of the War.

It was Christmas in 1953 when a series of photographs was commissioned to record some of the faces of the workers at Pease's Mill. This picture shows some of the ladies who worked in the Reeling Department. Crude but cheerful Christmas decorations have been put up on every available light fitting. This would send shudders through the body of any modern fire safety officer. It is perhaps surprising that the managers at the mill appear to have been so laid--back about the obvious risk; Pease's premises had had some bad experiences with accidental fires in the past. Their Leadyard Mill was destroyed by fire in 1817, and the Priestgate Mill nearby was the scene of a serious blaze in 1894 which caused 400 people to lose their jobs. Fire in one of Pease's adjoining warehouses, behind Darlington's Central Library, destroyed huge stocks of wool in 1933, and the mill itself was the victim of an incendiary bomb attack during the Second War. The mills which had provided so much employment in central Darlington eventually closed in 1972 and were pulled down in 1984.

The Hanking Room at Pease's Mill at Christmas 1953. The sign in the background proclaims "A Merry Xmas to All" and it is clear from the series of photographs taken at the time that the whole mill had entered the spirit of the festivities in a big way. The extent of the flimsy paper Christmas decorations hanging from every light is apparent again in this picture. It is amazing to see that this blatant fire risk was allowed. The combination of hot electric lamps, the dry paper and textile fabrics, not to mention the oil-soaked dry timbers throughout the factory was a recipe for disaster.

Below: The market hall steps, beneath the glass canopy, was the location of this historic photograph. It shows the Proclamation of the Accession of Queen Elizabeth II. The date was February 9th 1952. A detachment of soldiers can be seen below the Union flag and the steps are crammed with councillors and civic officials to give the occasion its due degree of gravitas.

It is said that at other times tramps would sleep rough on the steps of the market hall, wrapping themselves in the canvas stall covers in a bid to fend of the cold and damp.

Above: If you owned a uniform of any description when this photograph was taken, you were guaranteed a place in this procession... or so it seemed! Firemen, police, the military and many local organisations were represented here but sadly we are unsure of exactly what the occasion was. We can be fairly sure that it was taken in the 1940s or '50s, but there is an outside chance that it could relate to the coronation of King George VI in 1937. There were several other national celebrations over a period of around 20 years or so, all of which were marked by local events. The procession is seen passing the top of Tubwell Row and the base of the *town clock* and the market hall. This really does look like a major public event, with the whole town decked out in gaily coloured bunting and Union flags.

Left: Forster Street was the location for this picture which manages to capture the spirit of the celebrations in Darlington surrounding the coronation of Her Majesty Queen Elizabeth II. Above the window of the property in the picture is the royal coat of arms, together with official portrait pictures of the Queen and the Duke of Edinburgh. The royal couple were tremendously popular and the opportunity for ordinary people to express their support was grasped with a genuine eagerness. The coronation itself took place on June 2nd in Westminster Abbey. Several million people (though relatively few in the north of England) were able to see the ceremony for the first time on television. After the celebrations the Queen made her way to Buckingham Palace in a gold coach, cheered on by thousands of loyal subjects - many of whom had stayed up all night to see her. Scores of street parties were held in Darlington, the whole town being captivated by the glamour and romance of the grand royal occasion.

Below: Another happy scene celebrating the Queen's coronation, this time taking place along Brunswick Street. George and Maud Fawbert, Darlington legends at the time, are pictured here beside their barrel organ. George had the status of a likeable rogue and was well known to local council officials, the police and the courts. His contact with officialdom had more to do with his habit of bending the rules than any aspirations to serious crime. Born in 1874, he lived most of his life in Parkgate and ran many money making enterprises in the town. At various times he was a fish and mussel salesman, a property speculator, a coal merchant and a caravan park proprietor. In addition he ran a small bus service in the Darlington area as well as the town's first bicycle repair shop. George died at the age of 86 in 1960. Henry Ward and Violet Ward are dancing in the centre of the scene watched by some of their more inhibited neighbours.

Below: A cheery scene, made up almost entirely of men (though we can just make out two female figures on the left of the picture) which was recorded in 1937. The picture was taken quite near to Brunswick Street, and the residents have done a good job of erecting masses of bunting , flags and banners across the way to express their support and appreciation. One of the banners gives the game away - it reads 'God Save the King' so we can be fairly certain that the picture was taken to record the coronation celebrations at the crowning of King George VI. As a matter of interest, this was the first worldwide broadcast to be heard 'coast to coast' in the USA. 1937 was the year that Neville Chamberlain became Prime Minister, taking over from Stanley Baldwin. The Duke of Windsor married Mrs. Wallace Simpson, and the film *Snow White and the Seven Dwarfs* was released.

Right: A 1953 Coronation street party attended by the Lady Mayoress complete with chain of office and posh tea pot. The picture was taken as part of a series which ended up in one of the many newspaper 'commemorative specials.' Souvenirs of every description were created for the coronation which was one of the precious few occasions for public celebration in the first decade after the end of the war.

The residents of Brunswick Street were well known in Darlington for getting involved in national celebrations of all kinds with their organised parties and events. This childrens race was part of the series of events organised to celebrate the coronation of Queen Elizabeth II in Westminster Abbey in June 1953. The youngsters appear to aged around 9 or 10 on average, and that would put them in their mid-fifties at the time of writing. The scene could be taken from some post-war film about northern life in the 1950s, set as it is along the smoke-stained street in the shadow of the Darlington Power Station cooling towers. There was a lot of community spirit along streets like this one in Darlington at the time. It was an era when people would pop in and out of each others' houses and keep a watchful eye on their children when the need arose. Crime was at a low level relative to these days, and a stern look from a Bobby on the beat was usually more than enough to get the occasional bad lad back on the straight and narrow!

Right: People didn't have much in August 1945 when the *Victory in Europe Celebrations* captured the imagination of the country, but what they did have was shared with their neighbours' children at the street parties held around the district. An added sense of wartime Darlington is given in this picture by the camouflage covering the power station cooling tower, one of three at the end of the street. But now it was peace, at least in Europe, and the whole country was swept by a sense of relief and rejoicing, tinged of course by the inevitable sadness at the thought of lost loved ones who could not share in the victory celebrations.

It would have been an occasion these children

would never forget; the day that mam made them take the best table and chairs into the street for a party... and the man from the 'Echo got them to pose with Winston Churchill's well-known salute for the next morning's paper.

High Row was packed with royal supporters on 27 October 1952 when the Princess Royal took the salute from nearly 300 officers and men from the 50th Northumbrian Infantry Division Signals Regiment. The Princess had just unveiled a bookcase in St. Cuthbert's Church, built as a memorial to the brave men who had sacrificed their lives for their country. The service was attended by the relatives of the fallen heroes. Throughout the three hour visit the Princes swore the uniform of the Colonel in Chief of the Royal Signals. The royal party, including the Mayor and civic officials, went on to have lunch at the Drill Hall in Larchfield Street.

One of several royal visits to Darlington took place in October 1952. It was made by the Princess Royal. A group of young lads can be seen here lining the route that the Princess would take as she approached one of her engagements in Darlington. The visit involved a busy three-hour schedule, part of which saw the opening of the new Darlington YMCA in Park Street. She also unveiled a memorial to the soldiers of the 50th Northumbrian Infantry Division Signals Regiment in St. Cuthbert's Church.

Some of the lads shown here are wearing footwear which has seen better days, poor things, a mixture of tatty plimsolls, worn out boots and wellingtons. They look poor but happy, and it is worth remembering that more than a few things have improved since our childhood days. Keen eyes may be able to make out the sign on the right of the picture which shows the location of *Thomas's* the butcher.

A lot of men in suits, but precious few customers when this picture was taken at an exhibition held by Darlington Council in the 1960s. Every department of the Corporation was represented - from the Borough Architects Department to the Town Clerk's office. The library stand has the most visible stand in this scene, with a 'train' theme giving rise to the slogan "Follow your train of thought along these lines".... and "Your ticket to a first class service." In the 'Civic World' throughout the country in the 1960s there was a concerted effort to involve the community in the many changes which were being made at the time. No doubt this exhibition was part of a public information campaign being conducted by the Corporation.

Above: 1963 saw the visit of Her Majesty Queen Elizabeth the Queen Mother to the area. She had arrived to attend the celebrations at Darlington Grammar School. Always popular with the masses at any royal event, the Queen mum looks radiant and dignified here, despite the fact that she was 63 years of age when the picture was taken. A service was held at St. Cuthbert's, followed by lunch at the school. The party of school boys are lined up like a guard of honour here and are obviously impressed by the gravity of the occasion. Each will be approaching his 'fifties at the time of writing but we expect that the memory of the day *they met the Queen Mother* will be as fresh in their minds as ever. A few months after this picture was taken another memory would be etched on the minds of the youngsters here, for in November 1963 President John F. Kennedy was shot while on a visit to Dallas. Other events from 1963 include the notorious Profumo Affair, the Great Train Robbery, race riots in the USA and agreement being reached between France and Britain on the building of a channel tunnel.

At Leisure

The White Horse Hotel, Harrowgate Hill was the location for this picture. It was taken in January 1954 as part of a series of photographs produced for an exhibition of 'modern' hygienic food handling techniques. A new glass washing machine is being demonstrated by the lady behind the bar. The pipe-smoking customer looks reasonably impressed as the machine sprays each glass with scalding hot water and detergent. As if not entirely confident of the new technique, a note on the back of the print informed us that the glasses were washed every night by hand to make sure that they were entirely germ-free.

Left: This is a picture capable of striking the *nostalgia* chords and bringing back fond memories of the 1930s. The little girl is about to buy an ice cream from Mr Martino's ice cream tricycle. A cone would have cost her a halfpenny. She must have had a shy friend out of camera shot, as there are *two* dolls prams parked neatly on the footpath. The broad suburban street is Abbey Road, one of the well to do areas of Darlington. It certainly looks very clean and tidy in this picture. Mr Martino would sell ice creams in the warm weather and change to hot chestnuts and potatoes when winter arrived.

Below: It must have been chilly work in the lollipop-making department at this Darlington ice cream factory down at Feethams. In this photograph, another taken to demonstrate the high standards of hygiene in local food-handling establishments, lollipops freeze in their moulds and an operator places a stick in each one by hand. The photograph dates from 1954.

Left: The staff Christmas party at Henry Pease & Co. in a picture which is over 40 years old. The successful textile concern started by Henry Pease in 1752 occupied two town centre sites in Darlington. The East Street property was pulled down in the 1960s so that an indoor bowling alley could be built. It was demolished later to make way for a furniture retailers and a nightclub. The other site was cleared in the early 1980s and turned over to use as a car park.

Below: Another Pease's Mill Christmas scene. This time the employees children gather around the photographer to have their picture taken. This would be quite a novelty for the youngsters, most of whom, at the time of writing, will be heading for their 50th birthday. It is interesting to see how childrens' fashions have changed over the years; the little girls would, on the whole, not look too much out of place at a modern party in their smart dresses. But the situation with the boys is quite different. Try getting your little lad to wear a tank top, suit or short trousers.....let alone a tie! Towards the back of the room is the Christmas tree, and alongside it a notice board carries advertisements for chest X-rays and the 1948-50 National Service Act.

Darlington Rugby Football Club was founded in 1863 by the local Cricket Club members. With cricket being a summer sport the membership of the Club wavered during the winter months and it was proposed by a Mr TB Speciall that "a Football Club be established to supersede cricket during the winter months.....with the football played according to the Rugby Code.' Darlington Rugby Football Club was born.

The principle problems in the first two years of the Club's life lay with extending the playing activities to areas beyond the town's boundaries. Matches at Skerneside attracted followers but they were hardly very challenging. Local schools and colleges were, unsurprisingly reluctant to play against the town's side and there was no-one else in the district.

In 1865 the Club faced a crisis. during the Autumn, it received notice to quit its grounds on Park Street, just behind the Black Swan Public House, to make way for property developments. For reasons unknown the Club was given a year's grace and were offered to rent, two playing fields on the banks of the Skerne, the same fields that constitute the present cricket ground at Feethams. A series of fund raising events to pay for levelling and draining the swamp-like fields led to a growing awareness and interest in Darlington's new sport. This in turn led to extra income for the town's drinks and food sellers who brought their wares to the matches.

The Club grew more popular over the following years until 1877 when no records were kept until 1920. After the First World War, the Club was back in action by 1920, seeing a renewal of its record keeping and also a heightened success rate. In the inter-war years the Club produced several first rate County players, one of them was the late G Tarn

Bainbridge, who was elected President of the Rugby Football Union in 1975.

In August 1940 the Club's activities were suspended for the War and it wasn't until 1946 that play resumed at Hunden's Lane. In March 1952 the Club moved to a new eleven acre site at what was then Lingfield Lane (now McMullen Road). The ground was purchased for the Club by the president at the time, Arthur Feetham, and it was due to this one man's generosity that the Club was able to sell its assets there for retail development and move to its present site at Blackwell Meadows in 1994.

Above: Darlington Market Place c1880. The Bull's Head Pub on the right of the picture was a favourite haunt of the Club at the time.
Left: The River Skerne, along whose banks the Club played in the 1800s.
Below: The Park Street grounds were just behind the Black Swan Inn which is one of the oldest inns in Darlington.

Above: South Park in Darlington from a picture taken in 1929. The creation of the park resulted from a meeting of civic worthies, including Joseph Pease, in 1850. Money was put up by the group and the park was born. By 1877 the running of the facility was taken over by the Corporation. The boating lake came later, created in 1921 at a cost of £7,200. Some readers will have fond memories of courting days on the boating lake. Others will remember when dad allowed them to *take the oars* for the first time, and those first few uncertain strokes across the water. Readers would have to be getting on a bit to recall memories like this however, for the last boats to be hired in South Park were taken out of service over 50 years ago, in 1945! Less than ten years later the lake was filled in and a new course for the River Skerne created.

delightful thanks to the combination of mature trees with their heavy branches and broad leaves. Most Darlington people will have fond memories of days spent in the park. An all year round attraction, popular activities have included skating on the lake (rightly considered highly dangerous in modern times), sledging and boating or just promenading around the extensive footpaths beside the well kept flower beds.

Right: The playground in South Park was well attended when this picture was taken. The scene is

Above: This scene could have been taken from one of Enid Blyton's *Famous Five stories*. It shows a group of around a dozen children enjoying a 'good read' in the days before Australian soap operas, pop music and computer games ruled the roost. The fireside scene does look rather staged to the modern eye. It is thought to date from the 1950s and the caption written on the back of the print describes it as 'Fireside stories in the Juvenile Library.' The Juvenile Library was situated beneath the main library area in the Central Library and was popular with children eager to read the latest best selling adventure story. It is now used as a storage area in the library.

"...CHILDREN ENJOYING A 'GOOD READ' IN THE DAYS BEFORE SOAP OPERAS AND POP MUSIC RULED THE ROOST..."

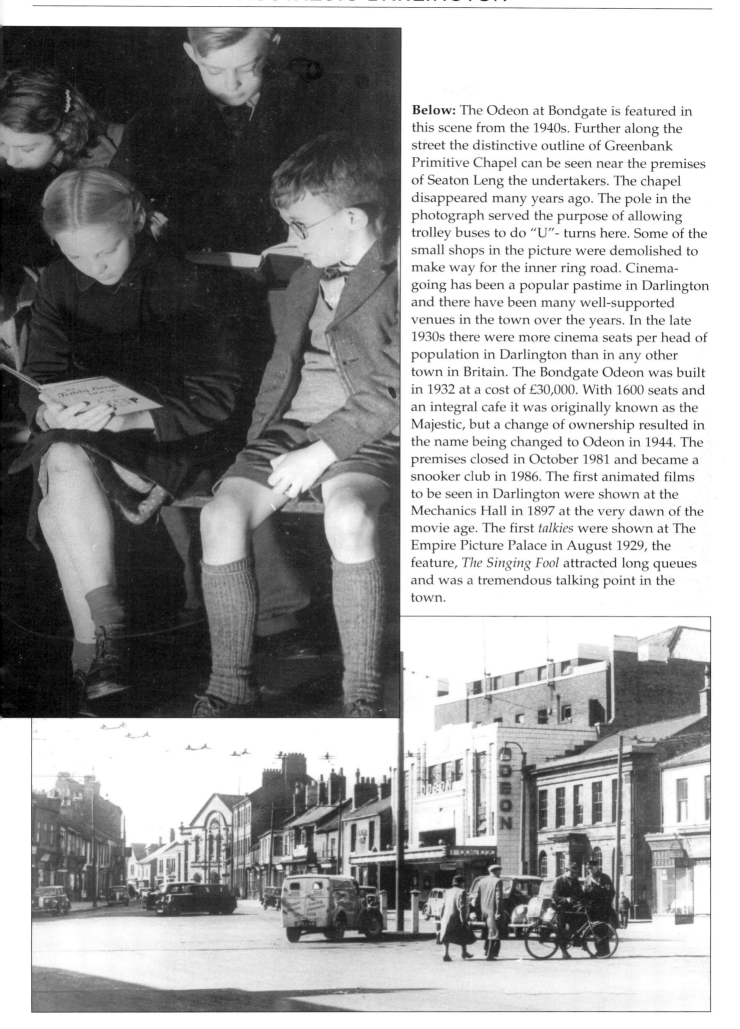

Below: The Odeon at Bondgate is featured in this scene from the 1940s. Further along the street the distinctive outline of Greenbank Primitive Chapel can be seen near the premises of Seaton Leng the undertakers. The chapel disappeared many years ago. The pole in the photograph served the purpose of allowing trolley buses to do "U"- turns here. Some of the small shops in the picture were demolished to make way for the inner ring road. Cinema-going has been a popular pastime in Darlington and there have been many well-supported venues in the town over the years. In the late 1930s there were more cinema seats per head of population in Darlington than in any other town in Britain. The Bondgate Odeon was built in 1932 at a cost of £30,000. With 1600 seats and an integral cafe it was originally known as the Majestic, but a change of ownership resulted in the name being changed to Odeon in 1944. The premises closed in October 1981 and became a snooker club in 1986. The first animated films to be seen in Darlington were shown at the Mechanics Hall in 1897 at the very dawn of the movie age. The first *talkies* were shown at The Empire Picture Palace in August 1929, the feature, *The Singing Fool* attracted long queues and was a tremendous talking point in the town.

Amdega - The result of ambition, determination and gain

For over 120 years, Amdega have been making fine timber conservatories in Darlington, County Durham, combining nineteenth century grace with twentieth century technology. These days conservatories are as fashionable as ever, but most people would be surprised at the aristocratic origin of what is now a popular home improvement .

The story begins in the days of the first Queen Elizabeth when explorers set out to discover new lands. Some of

them brought back strange and exotic plants which grew very well in their native countries but drooped and died in our climate - even in summer. Some form of protection was needed, for example, for the first known orange seeds that Sir Walter Raleigh brought back from America. Glass, which let in the light but kept out the frost and provided shelter from the wind seemed the obvious answer.

It was not long, of course, before there was a demand from some people to have such plants in their own gardens. Those who could afford it ordered small-scale, private 'hot-houses' or *conservatories.*

Sheltered growing conditions were

making even native English plants grow better. The rich considered these greenhouses and conservatories a highly desirable status symbol.

The Great Exhibition.
In 1851 the Great Exhibition was held in London. All the best examples of British manufacture were on show in an enormous glass-panelled structure, known, appropriately, as the Crystal Palace. It was designed by Joseph Paxton who was later knighted for his achievements. The 'Palace' made almost more impact than its contents and people began to see the possibilities of smaller versions of these glazed buildings in their gardens or as additions to their houses

William Richardson & Company is established.
Before long, everyone who was anyone wanted a conservatory and William Richardson & Company was established in Darlington in 1874 to take advantage of the new fashion by constructing greenhouses and vineries for commercial growers and private houses. They

Above: The company's first catalogue from the 1870s which contained monochrome pictures of the structures available.
Right: In 1905 Sir Robert Ropner MP. ordered a conservatory from Richardsons for his house, Preston Hall. This conservatory still exists and is the oldest example of the company's conservatory work in existence.

chose a site close to the London to Edinburgh line of the North Eastern Railway and built a large factory.

In the town best known to the rest of the country as the birthplace of the railways, the company was able to have its own sidings where trucks could be unloaded, re-loaded and sent off to do the contracted work. They carried all the required finished timbers, glass and building materials to finish a job. The workers who were actually to install the conservatory or greenhouse rode in carriages at the back of the train.

Spreading the word

Richardsons published a catalogue containing large pictures of every style of glass structure they had completed, to show how versatile they could be. Some were just simple porches but many of them were on a grand and elaborate scale. It is a mark of their good quality that many of them still stand today, including the conservatory at Preston Park, Stockton on Tees and the very splendid Palm House by the Ashton Memorial in Williamson Park, Lancaster.

There was also a short account of all the company's activities and all the services it offered. At the end of the catalogue, as a testimonial to their good workmanship, was a list of the company's recent clients who were largely members of the aristocracy and high society.

A new century beckons

The early 1900s saw the demand for Richardsons' conservatories continue to grow, with many prestigious orders gained at home and abroad. However, the onset of the Great War in 1914 meant a shift in priorities. Many firms with a manufacturing capability were required to help the war effort and this was the case with

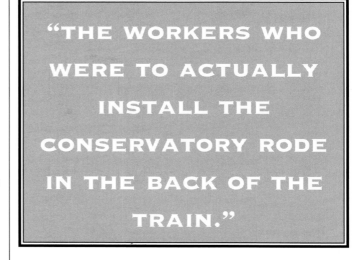

> "THE WORKERS WHO WERE TO ACTUALLY INSTALL THE CONSERVATORY RODE IN THE BACK OF THE TRAIN."

Richardsons, whose experience of high quality joinery was put to good use in the manufacture of bi-plane parts for the Royal Flying Corps, aeroplanes then being made largely from wood.

Between the wars

The end of the First World War enabled Richardsons to return to their normal work and the following decade saw their activities centred around satisfying the demands of their domestic and, increasingly commercial conservatory customers.

By the early 1930s, though, the world was becoming a different place and changing fashions, combined with the onset of the economic slump conspired to bring about a sharp decline in sales of conservatories to domestic households. For many businesses this would have been a terminal event, but Richardsons were an innovative firm and managed to stay afloat by using their expertise to gain business from local corporations for commercial *glass houses* - indeed, virtually every

Above: The original Amdega invoice dating from 1883.
Right: A span-roofed greenhouse, orchid-house or vinery from the first catalogue. Notice its continuous hinged top ventilating. These were erected in large numbers throughout Great Britain.

local corporation in the country became a customer at some time. Another string to Richardsons' bow, which became their saviour in the inter-war years, was the heating and ventilation service that the company offered, with no less than five of the country's cathedrals - Durham, York, Lincoln, Ripon and Southwell, benefiting from the installation of Richardsons heating systems.

Hostilities intervene again
The outbreak of war in

1939 interrupted normality for the second time. Although aeroplane parts were now made from metal, the woodworking skills that Richardsons had honed over the decades were again needed to help the national war effort. This time Richardsons' production swung over to the manufacture of sheds and other temporary buildings, which had to be quick to erect but strong and substantial to withstand the wide ranging demands made on them. Part of this work continued in a modified form after the war. The company made the 'Seco' type of pre-fabricated house which helped to relieve some of the immediate shortage of accommodation in badly bomb-damaged areas.

Richardsons remained in the joinery business and undertook contracts for the Ministry of Works, local education authorities and housing schemes.

"THE OUTBREAK OF WAR IN 1939 INTERRUPTED NORMALITY FOR THE SECOND TIME."

Post war progress
For some time after the war, timber was in very short supply. Making a virtue of necessity, Richardsons began producing greenhouses with aluminium frames. Heating systems began to be installed again in industrial and domestic premises. Also, Richardsons benefited from the reconstruction work that was available in British cities that had been heavily bombed during the Blitz.

Once peace was established and demobilisation released

Above: The cover for a catalogue of horticultural buildings and heating apparatus published in Belgravia Chambers in London. It gives the telegraphic address 'Richardson- Darlington'. The above picture dates from the turn of the century. Below: A conservatory erected in Hanley Public Park in Staffordshire in 1893.

the British workforce for their normal work there was a substantial increase in the demand for commercial greenhouses and conservatories. Richardsons were also offered contracts for work in schools and colleges as well as in hospitals.

The turning point

In 1963, a company change of name was decided upon. Amdega was chosen, a name that reflected the qualities on which the business had originally been built up, *ambition, determination and gain*. The name change co-incided with a rebirth of the fashion for domestic conservatories, though this time the reason was more practical. House prices had shot up. This meant that the addition of a conservatory to a house that had become too small for its occupiers was an ideal way of extending their living space. Orders rolled in and Amdega established itself as the leading company in the field.

After deciding in the mid 1970s to concentrate solely on high quality conservatory manufacture, by 1982 in the region of 400 conservatories a year were being made by a workforce of 66 people, with custom coming through a network of both agents and representatives.

Three years later demand had risen to a level that meant that additional space had to be found. Richardsons were fortunate in being able to buy land that adjoined their existing Faverdale site that had belonged to a steel stockholder. Machining operations moved in to the existing buildings and the company added a pre-fabricated office block to the front of the new premises. It was renamed Amdega 2. The new arrangements meant that improvements were necessary to the despatch area at the rear of Amdega 1. At the same time a building for timber storage and drying was erected at the back of Amdega 2.

Above: The front elevation of a conservatory erected for William Dingley of Camden Road, London.

Right: A conservatory with ridge-and-furrow roof. This building had a staggering 55 ft frontage.

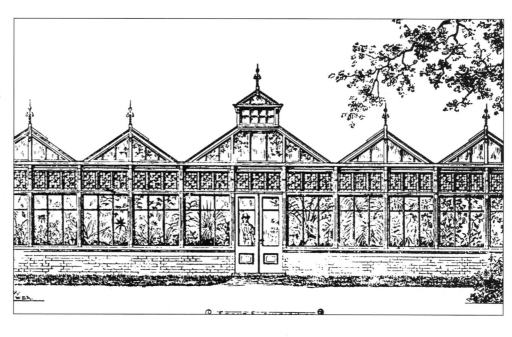

L F Knight was a long established Reigate firm who specialised in high quality summerhouses, gazebos and other garden buildings. Amdega took them over and the two companies together became Amdega Garden Buildings. Production from the new firm was transferred to Darlington in 1989 which proved a significantly successful year in Amdega's history. The machine shop (Amdega 2A) was extended, together with the nearby drying facility. Most importantly, though, this was the year that saw the first production from the recently built Amdega 4 factory. The largest number the company has employed at any one time was 500. Currently the staff numbers some 250 but modern methods are much quicker and more efficient. This means that a smaller staff is able to produce more conservatories in a year than ever before. But the fact remains that no two Amdega conservatories are the same, each is still 'tailor-made' in Canadian cedar to the exact requirements of the customer.

Above: Winter Garden erected at the Grand Hotel, Harrogate in 1906.

Right: A panoramic view of Preston Hall as it is today, the impressive workmanship that set the fashion in this country.

Today

The tradition of conservatory manufacture is now over 120 years old. It has served Amdega well and the current expansion into European and North American export markets means the future looks bright. Even in this modern, hi-tech

> ## "THE COMPANY NAME AMDEGA WAS DERIVED FROM THE WORDS AMBITION, DETERMINATION AND GAIN."

world people still appreciate the traditional skills that Amdega's craftsmen proudly exercise. Modern technology has a role in every business, but when it comes to making an *Amdega* conservatory, the methods, skills and sheer quality of workmanship are the same today as they were in Victorian times. The fact that so many of the original Richardson conservatories still provide good service to this day is testament to the wisdom of this policy

Ambition, determination and gain may be Victorian values, but this firm believes that they will be as relevant in the twenty-first century as they were in the nineteenth.

Above: *A craftsman shingling a cedar summerhouse roof.*
Below: *The final questions in designing a conservatory come when the building is finished. What about blinds? How should it be heated? These can be discussed with a qualified Amdega designer on site.*

Around the town centre

Right: A section of High Row in a scene dating from 60 or 70 years ago. From this elevated standpoint the major differences apparent at 'first glance' relate to the transportation of the day. The trolley buses (all single deckers in this view) and the spiders-web of overhead power cables indicate that the picture must have been taken after the 'trackless trams' were introduced in 1926. Taxis would ply for trade alongside High Row and many of their clients would come from the King's Head and visit the premises of local businesses and, of course, there would be frequent journeys to and from Bank Top station in the frail looking vehicles.

The most impressive building in this scene has to be that occupied by Barclays Bank, on the left of the picture. Further along the street the shop windows, including that of the London and Newcastle Tea Company, are protected from the sun by their traditional canvas shades.

Below: Northgate in the mid 1920s was the location of The Archer Rubber Company Ltd., among other businesses. In this picture they were promoting their *Keep-U-Dry Macks* in their 'alteration sale.' This picture gives a good view of the Prudential Assurance offices (which were built in 1911) and the Bay Horse Hotel.

Many people look at the street names of Darlington and assume that it must have been a walled town at one time, considering the number of 'gates' contained to the names of local streets. Most people know by now that the word *gate* is derived from an ancient word meaning street.

Bottom right: Tubwell Row as seen in a photograph taken in the mid 1920s. The most immediate indication of the age of the picture is the cobble stones complete with tram lines set within them. A trolley bus can be seen moving up Tubwell Row, away from the camera. At the time the picture was taken the vehicle would have had solid tyres, it was not until 1929 that more comfortable pneumatic tyres were fitted to every bus in the fleet. At around this time, in 1927, an experiment was tried with petrol-powered motor buses. Four vehicles were hired by the Corporation but the travelling public made so many complaints about the inferior level of comfort afforded by the vehicles that they were withdrawn. The last trolley bus ran in Darlington in July 1957. Tubwell Row has seen many changes over the years, one of the most dramatic and controversial being the construction of the glass and concrete buildings housing Barclays Bank and the Co-op in the late 1960s.

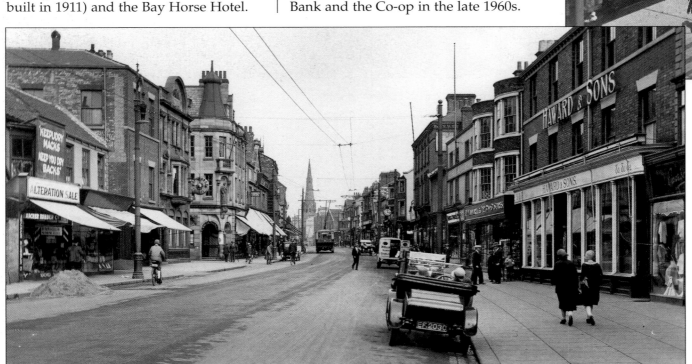

Above: This panoramic view of Darlington was captured from the Town Hall clock tower. The highest structure in the view is the spire of St. Cuthbert's Church. When the 150-ton spire was added to St. Cuthbert's the whole building sank some eight inches. The roof top of the covered market can be seen in the foreground, along with the businesses owned by White Brothers (motorcycle dealers) and Rose & Company. A clue to the date of the picture is seen on the right, taking the form of a group of charabancs involved in the business of excursions. This is not surprising, for the photograph was taken on Whit Saturday in 1936. The railway station is visible in the far distance, and the Dolphin Hotel and Waterloo Hotel can be seen on the right of the picture.

"WHEN THE 150 TON SPIRE WAS ADDED TO ST.CUTHBERTS THE WHOLE BUILDING SANK SOME EIGHT INCHES..."

Left: Some people may be surprised to see the *Dr. Scholl's Foot Comfort Specialist* shop on High Row in this picture which dates from 1926. The nearby Home and Colonial Stores outlet advertises the fact that they also had a shop at North Road. Interestingly, a horse van can be seen making deliveries alongside High Row, in between some of the early motorcars parked along the street.

Left: Skinnergate as seen in the early 1950s, in a view looking in the direction of the town centre. The Cameron Hotel on the right of the picture stood on the corner of Skinnergate and Duke Street. There was, at one time, a Halfords cycle and car accessories shop next door to it. Across the street Uptons operated their own cycle and radio shop - a strange combination perhaps to the modern shopper, but many cycle shops in Britain began selling wireless sets in the earliest days of the technology. The most famous of these, Currys, grew into one of the country's largest electrical retailing organisations from the most humble of origins. We shouldn't leave this photograph without a passing mention of the street lamp featured here. The stylish curved top had an unusual, small cube-shaped glass suspended beneath it - much more pleasing to the eye than the modern versions we see today.

Below left: This is how Northgate would have looked as you walked down it in 1926. This view was taken looking away from the town centre with the Bay Horse Hotel on the left. Bicycles were a popular method of transport at the time - there are at least six in view in this picture. The trolley bus, a single-decker, in the centre of the picture is the No. 19 destined for Harrowgate Hill. Some of the buildings in the scene have been replaced by modern retail structures which is a pity in many ways. F.W. Woolworths can be seen on the right of the photograph if you look carefully, with Melia's (the grocery store known for its keen prices) and Marks and Spencer further along the street. At the time this picture was taken Britain was gripped by industrial and economic problems, the most notorious of which being the General Strike which paralysed the country for nine days. The following year Al Jolson starred in the first talking film 'The Jazz Singer."

Below: Northgate, and a busy Darlington day in the late 1950s was chosen by the photographer when he recorded this scene. Trolley bus wires were still in place overhead when the picture was taken. Marinelli's ice cream salesmen was plying for trade along the busy street and we can see a lorry belonging to Shepherd's Fruit and Flower merchants further along the street. British Home Stores can be seen here next to Henderson's the Jewellers which, in turn is situated beside the Fifty Shilling Tailors. Westons is just visible between the Fifty Shilling Tailors and Alexandre. It was once a popular ladies dress shop. On the opposite side of the road Althams travel shop traded alongside a ladies hairdressing business.

Above: This almost historic scene from around seventy years ago records an un-posed view of daily life in the 1920s. The location is unmistakably High Row and it is pleasing to see that superficially at least the area has retained its original appearance. Of course, the overhead trolley wires disappeared in the late 1950s, more than 30 years after this picture was taken. The indoor market is featured strongly in this scene, as is *Binns* on the right of the view. The indoor market was open every day apart from Sundays and the Wednesday half-day closing, when trade would cease at 1.00pm prompt. The Home and Colonial Stores outlet can be seen on the left of the picture, the sign informs passers-by that they also had a shop situated at 11 North Road. The town clock dates back to 1864 and was designed by Alfred Waterhouse. The clock mechanism itself was made in York and paid for by Joseph Pease.

Below: This photograph dates from the 1930s and features the Bondgate area of Darlington. The scene was captured on a typical shopping day and features Fox's cafe on the right of the picture. Many Darlington people will have heard tales about the delightfully enticing smell which used to come from the freshly ground coffee produced at the cafe. Some more mature readers will remember it first hand. The combination of the aroma of freshly ground coffee beans and the chocolates sold at Moylers a little nearer the camera would have been tempting for any passer-by.

Fred Moses' shop on the corner of King Street supplied the soft furnishings for many Darlington homes over an extended period and some ladies may remember having their hair done at Raymant's next door.

Blackwellgate as it was around fifty years ago. The centre of the picture shows the popular local inn The Falchion, and nearer the camera the ladies outfitters Bainbridge Barker dominates the busy corner site. The 'Lotus' shoe shop and Sydney H. Wood the respected Darlington photographer were based between the two, opposite the newly installed traffic island which had been constructed to make it easier for pedestrians to cross here. Lower down the street saw the premises of Boots the chemist and Northern Goldsmiths. On the right of the picture the (new) County Hotel can be seen, and just beyond that N. Wilson and Sons were now running the business at the top of Houndgate. The County Hotel was built upon a site occupied by an older establishment of the same name. Its original name was the Black Bull and it was pulled down in 1956 to make way for the modern replacement which took only 90 working days to complete. One of the cooling towers of Darlington Corporation's power station can be seen in the distance. The Power Station was constructed in 1939, just before the beginning of the Second World War. Less than 10 years later the electricity industry was nationalised and control passed out of the local authority's hands.

Left: A picture set in the 1950s and featuring Tubwell Row. The selection of motor vehicles from the period adds a wealth of character to the scene. The truck on the far right of the picture is an ex-army vehicle, many of which could be seen serving local traders well into the '60s. Darlington's Public Museum is the building on the left, and opposite that is the Britannic Assurance offices (formerly the Savings Bank), alongside Darlington Car Mart and William Dodds the long established (1884) print seller and picture framer. The *town clock* keeps a watchful 'eye' on the comings and goings along the street, as it appears to do from many different angles on various pictures in this book.

Above: An unusual wide-angle view of the junction of Bondgate and High Row which manages to include many of the more architecturally-interesting buildings from days gone by in the same shot. Virtually in the centre of the view is the imposing structure housing Barclays Bank, with the Yorkshire Penny Bank on the right of it. There then follows Dunns and and Dressers the stationers, with the very ornate, but dignified Pearl Assurance building standing on the corner. Joseph Pease's statue had been moved about 20 ft away from the camera by the time this view was recorded and the installation of traffic lights had imposed a degree of order in the previously frantic flow of vehicles. The King's Head can just be seen on the left of the picture.

Right: Brinkburn Road in 1926. The growth of telephone ownership gave rise to the well used telegraph poles on the right of the scene, though gas lamps on the opposite side of the road remind us what the more typical technology of the day was like. The road surface looks wide and flat, but certainly not up to the job of coping with the rigours of the heavy traffic experienced today. It is interesting to reflect upon the news stories which would have been interesting to people back in 1926. The year saw the birth of our present Queen, the creation of the chemical giant I.C.I. and the establishment of the General Electricity Board.

Above: 1960s Darlington is represented in this photograph of Northgate. In the distance the Burtons building is shown, next door to Marks and Spencer. The growth of the Burtons tailoring empire throughout the country was tremendous in the 1930s when many of their characteristic stores with their imposing white facades were opened. Despite the ups and downs of the retail world, and the company has remained a major force in gents outfitting ever since. Northgate was popular with other gents outfitters too, for in the same picture the premises of John Collier and Alexandre the Tailors are shown.

It is hard to imagine the days before our town centre streets were overflowing with a tremendous variety of different kinds of food representing many countries in the world. We take for granted the burgers and pizzas, curries and kebabs. Less than 30 years ago the choice was much more limited, but one of the rare 'exotic' eating houses could be found on Northgate in the form of the Ying Hung Chinese restaurant. It is seen here, above and to the right of *British Home Stores.*

Below: Four Riggs, the narrow street off Bondgate, is featured in this view from the 1950s. The bakery business known as Bakewell Confectionery Ltd occupied the building on the left - note the ornate gas lamp fixed to the wall there, and a florists business stood opposite the narrow lane. In the distance it may just be possible to read the lettering on the 'Domestos Ltd' sign, denoting the location of the famous Darlington Chemical company which introduced one of the strongest brand names that the world of household bleach has ever known. The *Tyre House* was a tyre retailing business on Four Riggs that didn't quite achieve the fame of its neighbour, but nevertheless served the local motoring public well from these premises.

> **"BLACKWELLGATE WAS ONCE THE STARTING POINT FOR DARLINGTON'S FIRST OMNIBUS SERVICE.."**

Right: 1950s Blackwellgate is featured here. The Northern Goldsmiths clock is instantly recognisable near the delightfully fashioned street lamp on the street. Blackwellgate was once the starting point for Darlington's first omnibus service. Three strong horses pulled the vehicle from Blackwellgate to the railway station at North Road. It had a capacity of 41 passengers and fares ranged between 2d and 3d.

A spiders-web of overhead trolley wires dominates the foreground of this photograph which allows a Joseph Pease's eye-view of Prebend Row. The date of the picture is uncertain, but felt to be from around the mid to late 1940s. Of course, there have been many changes to the appearance of this part of Darlington since the picture was taken, but essentially the scene is instantly recognisable the heart of the town we know and love today. The ornate lamp stands seen here would be replaced by more effective but less pretty substitutes in the late 1950s, and the cobble stones which proved so slippery under foot and beneath the narrow tyres of the motors of the day would disappear too. The same fate awaited trolley wires, no longer needed of course after the last trolley bus ran on the streets of Darlington in the mid 1950s. An early Bedford articulated lorry can be seen in the picture, following the Domestos truck with its bull-nosed cab and Your Daily Help slogan.

Left: The point where Houndgate and Blackwellgate meet is featured in this photograph. It is thought to date from sometime in the 1930s and shows the large respected Bainbridge Barker Store on the left of the picture. Bainbridge Barker was Darlington's first department store, and was popular with the town's fashionable ladies for the quality and good value of the clothes sold there. Sadly it ceased trading here in 1961. Overhead power cables for the trolley bus system add character to the scene, as do the beautifully styled electric lamps which punctuate the busy street. Keen eyes may be able to work out the lettering on the small fishmongers' business on the right of the picture. It reads *S.A Morgan High Class Fish and Poultry*.

The Three Blue Bells public house is shown on the left of the picture. It found use as a collection office for parcels etc. when the Monday market carriers offered a delivery service in days gone by.

Below: April 1961, and the demolition men were out in force along Brunswick Street. This picture was taken looking in the direction of Borough Road. The tall chimneys and cooling towers of the Power Station can be seen in the background. They were to meet the same within 17 years. The 1960s saw a nationwide drive to improve the housing stock in Britain. It was a time when the poor quality victorian housing stock in many town centres was being pulled down and new council developments such as high-rise flats and suburban council estates were being built on their outskirts.

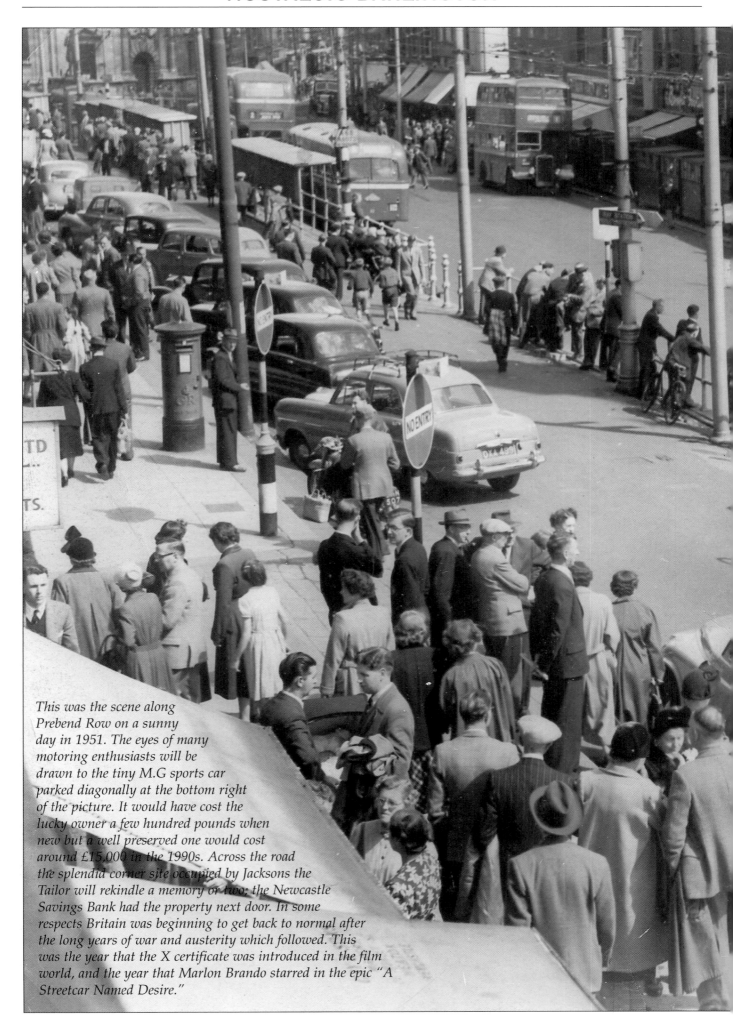

This was the scene along Prebend Row on a sunny day in 1951. The eyes of many motoring enthusiasts will be drawn to the tiny M.G sports car parked diagonally at the bottom right of the picture. It would have cost the lucky owner a few hundred pounds when new but a well preserved one would cost around £15,000 in the 1990s. Across the road the splendid corner site occupied by Jacksons the Tailor will rekindle a memory or two: the Newcastle Savings Bank had the property next door. In some respects Britain was beginning to get back to normal after the long years of war and austerity which followed. This was the year that the X certificate was introduced in the film world, and the year that Marlon Brando starred in the epic "A Streetcar Named Desire."

Above: A sea of carefully laid-out cobbles sweep around the corner at the junction of Northgate and Bondgate in this picture from June 1958. The top-left hand corner of the photograph contains the delicately designed arm of one of the old street lamps and the centre of the view shows a rather isolated Joseph Pease standing alone on his plinth in the middle of the junction. This could have been a picture taken to record the appearance of the King's Head Hotel, for it certainly does that perfectly. Or it could have been intended to show just how imposing was the bold, though stylish facade of the Midland Bank as the dawn of the new decade approached. Neither of these functions was the aim of the photograph, as it was taken as the planners were about to introduce changes to the junction which involved moving the statue of Joseph Pease and erecting traffic lights to control the traffic at this busy junction.

On the left of the picture the office of Taylor's Photographers can be seen, with the memorable rooftop message "When Baby Smiles...." The building was pulled down just a few weeks later.

Below: The new-look traffic junction can be seen here between Northgate and Bondgate. The date was September 1958. Many subtle changes had taken place in order to make the junction safer and to speed the flow of traffic through the town. It is difficult to appreciate the positive effect that traffic lights were to have on the traffic flow in the town, and the way they eased the load of the local police who had previously had the responsibility for directing the traffic at busy times. Here we see the statue of Joseph Pease in a slightly adjusted location, with an island of raised flags around him complete with protective railings. The cobble stones have gone, replaced by tarmac to afford better grip when the weather was unpleasant. Notice too that R. Blacket & Sons were in the process of rebuilding the shop which was formerly operated as a photography business by one Mr. Taylor for many years.

Above: Improvements, seen from outside the King's Head Hotel, to the junction of Northgate and Bondgate, soon after they had been completed. Joseph Pease's statue has been moved further away from the camera and a small pedestrian island has been constructed to make it safer for people to cross. The cobblestones have been removed and the whole area has taken on a more modern, streamlined appearance.

"THE PRESENCE OF THE 1950s MOTORCARS AND VANS ADDS TREMENDOUS CHARACTER TO THE SCENE.."

Below: Another view of the junction of Northgate and Bondgate from September 1958. It records the position of the traffic markings - such as they were, and Joseph Pease's statue before the alterations were made. The presence of the late 1950s motorcars and vans adds tremendous character to the scene. The style of the Pearl Assurance building on the corner of the junction seems to clash with the adjacent shops and businesses with their canvas sunshades and ordinary domestic-style windows above the plate-glass display windows at street level. Popular businesses seen here include Dressers, the stationers, Swaledale Cleaners and Johnson's the cleaners and dyers. The Midland Bank is just in view on right of the picture which is certain to evoke powerful memories of the Darlington we knew in the 1950s.

Above: The improved junction of Northgate and Bondgate, looking towards The King's Head. The King's Head was first mentioned in local records as far back as 1661, though it has been rebuilt since the original building first opened its doors to customers. The present hotel was re-styled in the 1890s with 50 bedrooms and stabling for over 30 horses. Unusually, the kitchens were located on the top floor of the hotel. This thoughtful measure was intended to ensure that the smell of cooking did not disturb the guests in their bedrooms. The tribute to Joseph Pease now has an area of flagstones around him, making it easier for pedestrians to get closer to the statue and harder for road traffic to get *too* close.

Below: A very nostalgic scene recorded in June 1958 at the Northgate/Bondgate junction in the heart of Darlington. Many elements in the picture add to the nostalgic feeling created by the photograph, the ornate lamp standard, the cobbled road and the delightful late 1950s motorcars and vans. The King's Head Hotel dominates the architecture in the photograph with the *Saxone* shoe shop, Maypole Dairies and Hepworths outlets beside it. On the right of the picture a *Swaledale Cleaners* delivery van is parked outside the business of the same name, no doubt waiting to set off on its rounds. Across the way we can just see the sign denoting the location of *Freeman Hardy and Willis'* shop and *Ekovision* further along the way. This photograph was taken to record the layout of this junction before traffic lights and a traffic island were introduced a week or two after the picture was taken.

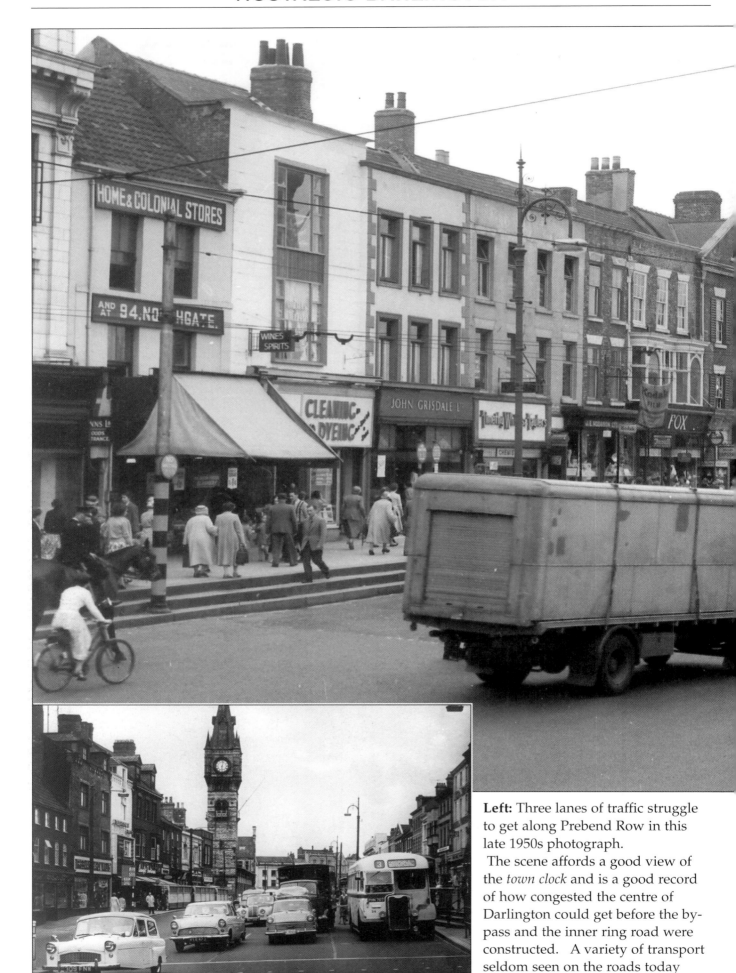

Left: Three lanes of traffic struggle to get along Prebend Row in this late 1950s photograph.

The scene affords a good view of the *town clock* and is a good record of how congested the centre of Darlington could get before the by-pass and the inner ring road were constructed. A variety of transport seldom seen on the roads today adds a degree of colour to the scene. The Bond three-wheeler on the left,

with its tiny 200 c.c Villiers motorcycle engine beneath the long bonnet, was entry-level motoring for many. Motorists a little higher up the scale could enjoy the quiet wallowing ride of the Ford Consul, seen behind the Bond in this picture. If the 'bus was your only choice then the characterful single-decker featured here, en-route to Faverdale via Woodland Road would have been just the ticket.

Above: A late 1950s shopping scene showing High Row and a queue of traffic waiting to pass through the town on its way to Durham and beyond on the A1. Delays and frayed tempers were often the consequence of congestion on the route through Darlington. The high volumes of traffic were a burden on the police, and their attempts to speed the flow of cars was a significant drain on their resources, particularly at holiday times. Several officers are shown on this picture, including a mounted policeman on the left. Traffic lights were a useful step in the right direction as far as solving the problem was concerned, and then the Darlington by-pass and improved motorway links transformed the problem permanently.

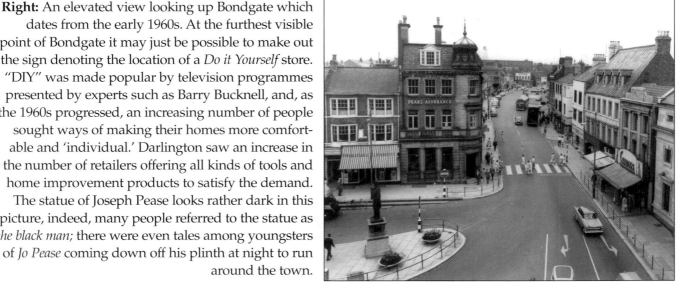

Right: An elevated view looking up Bondgate which dates from the early 1960s. At the furthest visible point of Bondgate it may just be possible to make out the sign denoting the location of a *Do it Yourself* store. "DIY" was made popular by television programmes presented by experts such as Barry Bucknell, and, as the 1960s progressed, an increasing number of people sought ways of making their homes more comfortable and 'individual.' Darlington saw an increase in the number of retailers offering all kinds of tools and home improvement products to satisfy the demand.

The statue of Joseph Pease looks rather dark in this picture, indeed, many people referred to the statue as *the black man;* there were even tales among youngsters of *Jo Pease* coming down off his plinth at night to run around the town.

A particularly pleasing wide-angle view of central Darlington which dates from 1962. It shows, of course, Horsemarket leading off to the right and High Row on the left. Many well-known landmarks can be seen in the picture, the most obvious of which being the town clock, and others including the covered market building, the old Town Hall, the Power Station and the spire of St. Cuthbert's Church. The main Darlington Post Office was once situated further along from the town clock but of course it now resides down Crown Street, a short distance from the Northern Echo offices. The photograph is interesting in the way that it records the skyline of Darlington as well as the buildings nearer to the camera in a way that cannot fail to rekindle pleasant memories. The old W. H. Smiths bookshop can just be seen on the right of the picture; unusually it had a tea room above it. The country's best-known bookseller moved to Northgate in 1970.

Left: The junction of Conniscliffe Road and Skinnergate, dominated by the imposing Darlington branch of Lloyds Bank Ltd. Above the bank the local administrative offices of the Liverpool Victoria Insurance company were located, characterised by their ornamental stone balconies. Around the corner the Northern Dairies self service cafe is seen, next to the motor insurance office operated by Thomas Hunter Ltd. The A67 to Barnard Castle is sign-posted to the left.

Below: W.H. Smith & Sons stood at the top side of Horsemarket when this photograph was taken in late 1950s. Bennett House, on the left of the picture, is worth a mention. On the right of W.H. Smith's is the ironmongery firm known as J. Lear and Sons. The long established ironmongery business ceased operating on this site in the mid 1960s... after 150 years trading.

Above: An elevated view looking towards the Midland Bank at the Northgate End of High Row. The Midland Bank dates from around 1920 - the York City and County Bank were demolished to clear a site big enough for the building and the opportunity to widen Northgate at this long standing bottleneck was taken at the same time.

The photograph was taken in 1969 and shows the congestion that was largely caused by the number of buses picking up and setting down their passengers along this stretch. A hoarding advertising cigarettes for 4s 6d for 20 can be seen on the left of the picture.

In the days when all the north and south-bound traffic was routed through the centre of Darlington it could be quite a job to get across some of the town centre streets. This scene was recorded along High Row and shows a police officer holding up the traffic so that this group of people can cross safely on the zebra crossing. This crossing had Belisha Beacons positioned on it in order to alert oncoming traffic of its position. These bright orange lights took their name from the Minister of Transport at the time of the 1930 Road Traffic Act, Mr Hore-Belisha.

At war

Below: War work in progress at the Darlington Locomotive Works. Here we see women busy "in the shops" on a damp day during the Second World War. Components for armaments are being transported by a 'Lister Auto Truck' in this 1940s scene. The Lister truck was basically a heavy diesel engine mounted on a short chassis and used for towing small trailers around the yard. The high centre of gravity meant that it was not renowned for its good handling characteristics, but its tight turning circle meant that it was ideal for guiding heavy loads in and out of the tricky spaces in the works.

Above: An historic scene. The first Darlington Postwomen, pictured outside the General Post Office building in Crown Street. The photograph dates from May 1941 and some of the names of the six ladies are known. They are, left to right, Sally Craggs, Nora (surname unknown), Cathy (surname unknown), Winnie Harrison, Mary Watson and Jennie Blows. Clearly, these ladies, like many others, had been drawn in to the postal service by the demands of the war. Britain, unlike Germany, was living under a siege economy during wartime. The State in the U.K had far-reaching involvement and control of the daily lives of her citizens. Germany, on the other hand, never fully mobilised women to help with the war effort. From May 1940 control of manpower (and *woman* power) rested in the hands of Ernest Bevin, Minister of Labour. It was predicted that a million and a half women would be needed to help with the war effort. This included all aspects of engineering, public services and agriculture. It was compulsory for women to register for war work from March 1941 and eventually all women between the ages of 18 and 60 were registered. For most, if not all women, war work was welcomed. It offered guaranteed jobs with decent money and a sense of pride and purpose that had been lacking in some women's lives in pre-war days. There was the opportunity to take on responsibility, have fun and make new friends too as everyone worked together to defeat the Nazis.

Above: The Darlington Spitfire was purchased through the fund-raising efforts of local people in the Second World War. Throughout the war there was a series of tremendously powerful fund-raising campaigns aimed at raising money for warships, fighter planes, tanks, comforts for the troops and so on. There were savings-bond schemes and campaigns to recycle scrap metal, newspapers and virtually anything else which could be salvaged and re-used. This resulted in the disappearance of the railings from around many houses, schools, churches and parks - all to be melted down and turned into weapons and equipment. The Spitfire featured here was the pride of the town, and cost £55,000. Fighter aircraft were based at the wartime aerodrome at Middleton St. George, the facility initially staffed by Canadian Airmen who became regular visitors to Darlington during the war. The airfield closed in the 1960s.

Below: This enormous tank rumbled through the town centre as part of the 1947 Victory Parade in Darlington. It is seen here passing Minories Garage and the shop owned by G.W Thomson. The Mayor took the salute at High Row as the streams of military and voluntary personnel marched past. Rousing music was provided by the combined bands of the Hussars and the Guards.

"THE MAYOR TOOK THE SALUTE AT HIGH ROW AS THE STREAMS OF MILITARY AND VOLUNTARY PERSONNEL STREAMED PAST.."

Above: This parade is thought to have taken place in June 1944 and was probably part of the Mayor's Sunday procession of the time. The premises on the left of the picture were the home of Atkinsons, the cabinet makers and upholsterers established in 1934.

If the date on the back of the original print is accurate, the picture was taken just four days after the Normandy landings in France. This was one of the biggest logistical events of the war, with 700 ships and 4000 landing crafts taking part in the operation which would lead to eventual victory over the Nazis. It was also around the time that the first flying bomb (V1) dropped on London, but in the country as a whole there was a sense that the end of the war was in sight, apparently confirmed by the relaxation of blackout regulations.

Below: This was the scene on Northgate in June 1946. Rather primitive-looking tanks can be seen rattling and rumbling though the streets of the town centre as part of the Victory Celebrations.

The white building in the background is Minories Garage - they sold vehicles from the now defunct Rootes Group, such as Hillman, Sunbeam Talbot, Commer and Karrier. Further along the road is the old billiard hall at Corporation Road.

There was obviously much to celebrate at the end of the war, but the celebrations were tempered with sadness, as virtually everyone knew of someone who had been killed or badly injured in the war. The remainder of this decade would see some tough economic times as the country struggled to get back on its feet. The Bank of England had been nationalised in February 1946 and bread was rationed just a month after this picture was taken. Later the same year the National Health Service was formed, but there were difficult times around the corner for the British economy which would affect the lives of the people of Darlington in the years which followed.

CIVIL DEFENCE

CIVIL DEFENCE
IS COMMON SENSE
IT CONCERNS YOU

DARLINGTON COUNTY BOROUGH CONTROL I 2 H

Above: Civil Defence was the big issue in the late 1950s and for much of the 1960s, as fear of nuclear war pre-occupied the western world. Plans were set in place throughout Britain to ensure that public order would be maintained in the event of the national government being disabled by an overwhelming nuclear attack from the East. Underground bunkers were identified from where small teams of civic officials would co-ordinate attempts to restore public health, public order and the rebuilding of the community in the event of a nuclear strike, as well as being the link with the outside world and whatever might be left of central government. Relationships between the *Super Powers* were at a low ebb; this was the era of the Cuban Missile Crisis (1962), the Berlin Wall (1961) and a series of high profile East-West spy scandals.

Left: A proud day for Darlington. April 22 1947 saw the visit to the town by England's greatest military war hero of the day, Field Marshal Viscount Montgomery, as part of the Victory Celebrations which took place throughout Britain. This picture shows 'Monty' inspecting the troops, accompanied by their rather anxious commanding officer and the Mayor of Darlington.

The seasoned soldier was incredibly popular, as can be seen from the fact that every vantage point was crowded with people desperate to catch a glimpse of their hero. Note the people crowded on the balcony in front of Mason's cafe, entirely typical of the lengths people went to in order to see what was going on. As part of the visit to Darlington the Field Marshal unveiled a portrait of Winston Churchill in the entrance to Darlington Library above a Victory Panel to commemorate the sacrifices made during the war. It can still be seen there to this day.

Above: Crowd control was clearly top of the agenda when Field Marshal Montgomery visited the town in 1947. The crowd was good humoured and determined to express their support and gratitude to the popular war hero as he walked smartly and confidently around the town centre. In this picture *Monty* can be seen following the Mace Bearer, with the Chief Constable of the Darlington Police Force, the Mayor and other civic officials. The crowd must have been large judging by the officers in the background with their linked-arms. The party was moving away from High Northgate and people can be seen leaning out of the upper window of the Prebend Library on the right of the picture. Montgomery's visit was made during the official celebrations to mark the end of war.

Wheels of time

Above: A shiny new diesel train awaits its passengers at Darlington station in the 1960s. The destination was Saltburn, and in the days before family holidays to Majorca were commonplace, a day out to the seaside at Saltburn or Redcar would have been the highlight of the school holidays. No book about Darlington would be complete without a mention of the railways, for it was in our district that the railway age began and spread to the four corners of the world. The Bank Top station we recognise today dates from 1887. It replaced a rather tatty wooden structure which simply failed to do justice to Darlington's place in the history of railways; the building was even criticised by Queen Victoria when she visited the town in 1849. the new station was built at a cost of £110,000 by the Great North of England Railway Company.

Right: A gloomy but dramatic scene showing clouds of steam and smoke in the area around the Power Station, beside the main railway line in Darlington. It was taken from the Haughton Road Bridge sometime in the late 1950s. The mixture of steam engines and the dramatic, tall concrete chimneys makes a memorable sight. The concrete chimneys stood over 250ft tall - almost 100ft taller than the adjacent cooling towers, in an attempt to limit the amount of pollution settling on the town.

Right: A memorable view of a trolley bus as it climbs the hill towards Prebend Row in Darlington. The vehicle in question is a Leyland 304 with central passenger access which first saw service in November 1940 and continued in use for thirteen years until November 1953. The vehicle was heading towards Prebend Row where it would have unloaded its passengers on the busy street. This part of the town has, of course, changed dramatically since this scene was recorded and many of the buildings that the trolley bus had passed on this section of the route have now been pulled down. Kent and Brydon's the popular florists had an outlet here which will be remembered by many local people. The business was established in the 1870s and traded from their Horsemarket premises up until 1971. The *Savings Bank* was nearby. Many of the buildings were swept away to make room for the Cornmill shopping development.

Below: A row of trolley buses lined up for a photograph in 1943. Darlington was one of the first towns in the country to operate a trolley bus service. The first public transport service available on the streets of the town was based on steam-driven trams. It began in 1862 and was known as the Darlington Street Railroad. After just three years the firm ran into difficulties and horse drawn trams eventually took the place of the steamers. The first circular trolley bus route was introduced in 1928 and ran from outside the Midland Bank, going as far as Auckland Road. Initially 24 vehicles were employed on the service. The trolley buses were phased out in the 1950s, the service to run being in July 1957. By June 1958 all the paraphernalia associated with the network had been dismantled.

Bottom right: This Corporation Transport double-decker trolley bus, registration number LHN 783, is seen loading passengers at Low Flags, outside Dunn & Co. the hat makers. More mature readers may remember the distinctive sign above the shop which was designed, not surprisingly, in the shape of a hat. The vehicle seen here had Leyland running gear beneath the body constructed at East Lancs motor body works. The picture is thought to date from 1949. It is hard for us to imagine, in modern times, the complexity of creating an urban transport system which relied upon rigging electric overhead cables above many miles of the town's busiest streets and roads. Despite the interruptions to the service caused by the trolley poles coming adrift from the overhead wires, the vehicles were popular. They made a big difference to the quality of the air in the centre of town as they generated virtually no pollution, unlike their smoky diesel-engined counterparts.

Above: A thought-provoking scene from the 1930s which gives a real impression of what Darlington town centre life was like in that era. Northgate was the setting for the elevated view, and a heavy load of steel troughing on the back of a lorry, operated by John Coxon of Elswick in Tyneside, can be seen holding up the traffic and causing a long queue as it approaches the camera. To the left of the struggling truck is a single-deck trolley bus, making its way along Northgate and no doubt hoping that the twists, turns and junctions in the town centre will not dislodge the delicate trolley poles above it, upon which it relied for its motive power. The light coloured corner site on the left of the picture was occupied by Bell and Rayner Ltd., house furnishers for many decades in Darlington and a name recalled with affection by many local folk. Althams the travel agents were located next door to Bell and Rayners, and a ladies hairdressers was situated a little further down the street, around thirty yards before the welcome entrance to the Bay Horse, seen here advertising its *buffet* eating facility. At the top right of the picture it is just possible to discern the letters on the sign of British Home Stores department store.

Below: The traffic policeman, or point-duty policeman as he would be more accurately described, is fighting a loosing battle on Grange Road in the early 1950s. The traffic here is south-bound, and more mature Darlington residents will recall with horror the chaos which would regularly hit the town each summer when the growing volume of holiday traffic would pass through it, with people en-route to their favourite holiday resort. Further along the street it is just possible to make out the sign of the *Palais de Dance.*

Above: The construction of this new section of ring road around Darlington would have been one good reason to record this scene. It dates from 1960 and gives a good impression of what this end of the town looked like with the gas holder in the distance. Much of the property in the distance has been pulled down since the picture was taken.

Below: Darlington by pass made an incredible difference to life in the town. It enabled 'local' and 'through' traffic to be separated and reduced the irritating delays which had characterised journeys through the town - especially during the summer holiday periods. The construction of the A1 M west of Darlington was completed in 1964. Further moves to prevent the 'competition' between through traffic and local traffic occurred later when town centre ring roads were built. Often controversial, because of the need to pull down shops and houses, the ring road was an essential element in the modernisation of the town centre. In a survey conducted in 1977 it was found that the A66 carried a staggering average of 19000 vehicles per day, of which 3000 were heavy goods vehicles. It is clear that we are a long way away from solving our problems on the over-used systems at present as anyone who drives near to the town centre on a Saturday will confirm, but we have made at least some progress since the A1 used to pass through our main streets.

Seven decades of Ford in Darlington

In 1926 a car dealership was founded by John Neasham at Parkgate, Darlington. Two years later the Ford franchise was awarded and the company prospered, even through the Second World War when the emphasis was on the servicing of tractors for farming to help the war effort.

In March 1965, work began on a £135,000 new building scheme. The new garage included showrooms, petrol station and car-wash.

It extended from Brunswick Street to Stone Bridge roundabout and, in the Northern Despatch, was referred to as "the first trend-setting new building"

> **"WORK BEGAN IN MARCH 1965 ON A £135,000 NEW BUILDING SCHEME."**

on the Darlington Inner Ring Road. It caught the eye with its exterior of glass and aluminium curtain walling. The work was done by Edgar Lawson Ltd. and the architects were Messrs H.B. Richardson of Skinnergate.

The new and more spacious accommodation made an increased workload possible and within two

Left: During the war, the emphasis was placed firmly on the supply of tractors for the farmers in the area.
Below: A delightful 1960s picture of the showrooms with the Ford Anglia clearly the star of the show.

Farmers have been warned!

JOHN NEASHAM,
THE HOUSE FOR FORDSON TRACTORS

Many good and substantial reasons are supported by actual facts in the contemplation of the unusual values offered in Fordson Tractor Services today. It is true that new methods usually produce greater service facilities. Messrs. John Neasham, Parkgate Garage, Darlington, and Northallerton Motors, South Parade, Northallerton, have a staff of Fordson Tractor Experts. Our Stores at both Depots are a revelation in efficiency, housing a comprehensive stock of genuine Fordson Spares and other accessories such as Lister Cockshutt Plough Parts including Third Furrow Extension, Fuel Tanks, and recommended grades of oil for your Fordson. Our Service Depot is one of the finest equipped in this part of the country, instantly ready to give attention to your Tractor, whether it is just a minor repair job or a complete overhaul. WHEN IN NEED 'PHONE DARLINGTON 2107, 2247, or NORTHALLERTON 247. WE DO THE NEEDFUL.

years a further 20 staff were appointed, bringing the total number of employees up to 185.

In 1966, with dealerships at local Richmond and Northallerton, the move to the new site was completed. This location on St. Cuthbert's Way was in fact the site of the first Methodist meeting in Darlington in 1753 and to this day a plaque exists that was set up to mark it.

In 1969, however, the business foundered and was taken over by the Skipper group. They, in turn, were

taken over by the present owners, Harrogate-based Sanderson Bramall Motor Group plc in 1993. Today, as Sanderson Ford, the company still represents Ford and indeed, it is taking a larger territory for Ford product throughout North Yorkshire and South Durham.

Above: A 1980s picture of the showrooms on St. Cuthberts' Way.
Top: The same premises in the 1960s with the distinctive cooling towers in the background.
Left: A charming 1960s array of Ford vehicles in the showroom of Sanderson Ford.

Shopping spree

Below: How many of us can remember our parents buying us an ice-cream from *De-Luca's* or *Dipaolo's* when we were young? In many households it was almost a bribe to ensure good behaviour as the youngsters were trailed around the market stalls, with mothers looking for bargains or some elusive item of clothing. More cunning parents arranged to buy the ice cream *after* the walk around the stalls on the condition that good behaviour had *been* achieved. In this picture we see the market in full swing, with a few stalls shielded by the overhead glass canopy and others taking their chance in the open market area. On the left of the scene Rose and Company sold wallpaper and paints to eager clients and facing the camera, beyond the market stalls, the Broadway Cafe, The Waterloo public house and The Hole in the Wall public house can also be seen.

Above: Market Place Darlington, and shoppers are seen going about their business, seemingly oblivious to the work of the photographer. The Boot and Shoe Hotel with its questionable tudor-style facade is visible just left of centre, and behind that the cooling towers of the power station can also be seen. The sharp confident spire of St. Cuthbert's rises above the traders, just as it had done over similar market scenes for many centuries. There can be little doubt that even after a period of 900 years the church remains at the top of the list of Darlington's most impressive buildings. During the first 500 years of its life it was the only public place of worship in Darlington. This *monopoly* ended when the Society of Friends opened their first local meeting place in 1689. Like so many similar buildings in towns and cities up and down the country it is all too easy for local people to take St. Cuthbert's for granted, so why not spare an hour or so to revisit it?

Left: Mid-afternoon chaos, or so it seemed. It often did get chaotic along the main route through Darlington, after all, this was the usual path taken by traffic heading up and down the east side of the country along the A1 in the days before the motorways and the Darlington by-pass. To be fair the congestion in this picture seems to come more from the pedestrians than the motorists - and note how the cars were allowed to park at 45 degrees along High Row. Some familiar business names can be seen in the picture, including Timothy Whites, (formerly Taylors the chemist and later to merge and become *Boots*) Collingwoods and John Grinsdale on the left. At the bottom centre of the picture a British Road Services lorry can just be seen as it approaches the camera. The drab green coachwork of these vehicles was a common sight on local roads in the 1950s and '60s, much to the annoyance of independent haulage contractors who felt under pressure from unfair, restrictive transport regulations and the threat of nationalisation of the road haulage industry.

Bottom left: The much-photographed Tubwell Row, this time in a picture taken in the early 1960s. By this time the rebuilt Nags Head on the left of the picture has taken on a modern look in order to further the sales of its Worthington Beer. Many town centre drinkers were sad to see the *old* Nag's Head demolished - it had served the town since the seventeenth century and was pulled down in order to erect the new version in 1962. The Darlington Museum is on the left of the picture, below the Nags Head. Tubwell Row is one of the town's most historic streets. At one time sheep pens would be erected along the right hand side of the street on market days. The street was named after a water well which was located here and referred to in public records as far back as 1545.

Below: Northgate in the 1960s. Alexandres store is on the right of the picture with the Army Information Centre above it. Further along the street is British Home Stores - they had been trading in Darlington since 1935. Across the street a new retail property offering TV rentals had been constructed which replaced a large three-storey building which had stood there for over a century.
In later years the Queen Street shopping arcade would transform the appearance of part of this area, as the demands of the large retail chains caused the construction of purpose-built shop units.
The spire of Northgate United Reformed Church can be seen in the distance, virtually in the centre of this view.

Above: The sign on the Radio Rentals shop on Skinnergate was big and bold. The picture was taken from the Grange Road end in 1963. This was the place to buy (or rent) your T.V or radio, and the shop window crammed with the most up-to-date radio and T.V sets would have been a tempting sight to passers-by. It wasn't really until the 1960s that T.V ownership began to take off in the north of England but demand had been rising steadily since the Coronation in 1953.

Further along the street *Snowballs* can be seen. It will be remembered as a popular but inexpensive ladies outfitters.

Left: Post House Wynd is featured in this rare photograph. The street takes its name from the Posting House which used to operate during the last century from the Talbot Hotel. The Talbot was pulled down in 1902. We have a fair idea that the scene was captured at 1.00pm thanks to the clock above A.E. Hopper and Sons jewellery shop. Ideal Fisheries is shown slightly further up the street, near to the Expresso Coffee bar. Coffee bars were a product of the late 1950s and '60s. Many had their own juke boxes and were a magnet to youngsters drawn by the dual attraction of frothy coffee and the latest pop music. The large sign shown on the building on the right of the photograph marks the location of "Winterschladen & Co. Wines and Spirits Merchants" - we can appreciate why it had to be a *large* sign! The Green Dragon deserves a mention too for its long service to thirsty town centre drinkers.

Above: The Market Place and a sea of canvas stall roof-tops can be seen in this early 1960s view. The picture was taken from the market hall steps and shows shoppers and bargain hunters at work in the crowded arena below. The ornate pillars holding up the glass canopy around the covered market can be seen clearly in this picture. They were added to the original structure to cater for the demand for sheltered sites for stalls in 1885. Virtually in the centre of the photograph Cowan's *Orion Snackbar* is visible; it was well known for the quality of the hot tea, coffee and sandwiches capable of rejuvenating the most weary of cold traders and shoppers when the need arose. It was a welcome oasis and meeting point for local people en-route to a serious shopping session. The bus station at Feethams, completed in 1961, is in the distance.

Left: Market trading in Darlington can be traced back over many centuries. The Bishop of Durham first granted a charter for the purpose of organised market trading in the town in the twelfth century. At one time the open space created by the *market place* was the only central place available to meet and hold meetings and other events. It has therefore seen several different historic occasions over the years, including at least one public execution!

Above left: Another view of a busy market day. The premises of T. Pease and Co. the wines and spirits merchants can be seen on the right of the picture, and a good view can be had of the distinctive glass-roofed border of the market - a later addition to the original building designed to exploit the demand for even more under-cover trading space. The Volkswagen van in the foreground makes the picture look rather later than it is - these vans began selling in decent quantities from the early 1960s and later models retained largely the same appearance right up until the late 1970s. The vehicles never came close to matching the popularity of Ford's Transit vans, many of which would have been the trusty workhorses of the traders working here.

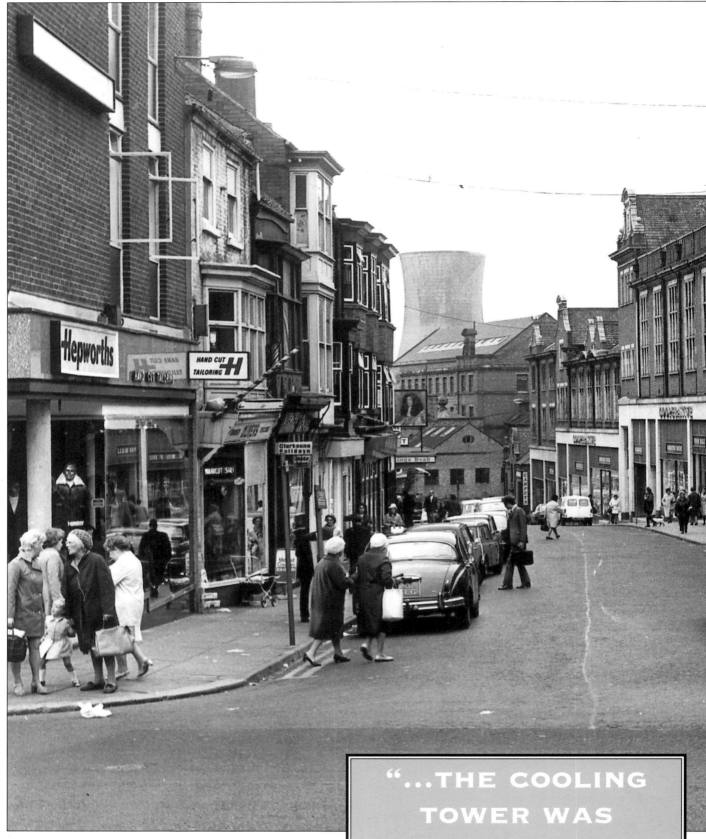

Above: A view down Priestgate from Prebend Row in the early 1970s. Note the cooling tower in the background - it was demolished in 1978 along with the rest of the power station. The Co-operative department store can be seen just right of centre in this scene. The building was pulled down in 1988 to make way for the Cornmill shopping development.

"...THE COOLING TOWER WAS PULLED DOWN IN 1978 WITH THE REST OF THE POWER STATION"

Below: An early 1950s view of Blackwellgate, looking west. The picture gives a nostalgic view of a typical shopping day in the centre of town. Binns and Co, *House Furnishers* is the large store on the right of the picture, Sydney Wood the photographer ran his shop a little further along the street. His wedding photography service was known not to be the cheapest in the area, but it was considered to be one of the best by those with an eye for a decent picture. Wood was the official photographer for many Darlington Mayors during his career. Even further along Blackwellgate was Boots the (*cash*) chemists and the Northern Goldsmiths shop, complete with its familiar *Rolex* sign outside it. The lovely ornate lamp stand is worthy of a mention. They would have cost more to produce and maintain than the soul-less concrete lamps which replaced them, but the difference they make to the appearance of the street was surely worth it.

Bainbridge Barkers was on the corner in the distance, opposite the School Furnishing Company which supplied schools and libraries throughout the north for many years until the company transferred its business to Peterborough in 1963.

Right: Darlington Market was guaranteed to draw the crowds on a Whit Monday, as it was one of the few markets to be open for trade on Bank Holidays. People would come from many miles around to buy a bargain or just browse around and enjoy the atmosphere. There are plenty of people in attendance here, and the curvaceous Bedford ice cream van looks to be doing a steady trade. The building on the right belonged to T. Pease and Sons Ltd., and the Williams Piano and Radio shop occupied the building directly in front of the camera, some distance away. The picture looks rather recent at first glance, and it is difficult to believe that it is almost 40 years old. Market shopping has been an important part of Darlington life for centuries and with a little luck will continue to be so.

Below: A sea of heads surrounds a pair of street entertainers on a Darlington market day. Goodness knows what the 'act' in question was, we can see that it involved wearing a fez and a blindfold, but it certainly drew the crowds. In the distance, to the right of the Boot and Shoe hotel, we can see the cooling towers of the power station. To the right of the cooling towers is St. Cuthbert's Church. Before the war the open market would open just on Mondays - and was unusual in that it would open for trading on Bank Holiday Mondays too, attracting thousands of shoppers from all over the district.

Bottom right: A view of looking across Darlington town centre towards the *town clock,* in a picture taken from the new Town Hall. The scene dates from August 1972. On the left of the picture, in the distance, the distinctive roof of the old town hall is visible. This Victorian building was constructed between 1861 and 1864 as part of the market complex. The market can be traced back further than almost anything in the town. The covered market came later and cost just over £16,000 in 1863. Darlington became a Municipal Borough a short time later, in 1867, and a County Borough in 1915. By 1938 the covered market had 37 butchers stalls, 15 poultry dealers, 35 green-grocers and no less than 6 florists.

The steps along High Row are seen completely occupied by men during the Cleveland Bridge strike. The Saxone Shoe shop is shown - the well-known shoe retailer had traded in Darlington since 1916. High Row has been the location of many gatherings, meetings, and marches over the years, as well as the location of some of the town's most respected and longest established businesses and banks. Dressers the stationers in a good example - after being established in 1846 they have remained on High Row, despite a relocation which saw them move just a few doors along the street.

NO ENTRY

Cold comfort for Darlington

In the years before the war, when wages were low, the ship building and mining towns of the Tyne and Tees used to be spoken of as 'a depressed area'. It was an accurate description at the time but a thriving post war economy did much to change it.

In the frozen food industry too, growth and industry were key words. Though people in the north east took to the frozen product with a little less eagerness than Londoners, their resistance was steadily worn down.

In the Tees-side area, the Darlington firm of Shepherd & Company Ltd. was the main wholesale distributor of frozen food since 1948 and have been known in Darlington as wholesale fruit and vegetable merchants since 1848.

Right and below: Strawberries for sale (right) brought from Covent Garden and collected from the railway station by the horse and cart below. This was one of four purchased when the business was first founded to collect produce from London at the Darlington Railway Station.

John Francis Shepherd, originally a farmer, who died in 1932, established his company in 1884. To begin with its business was selling potatoes but then it diversified into fruit and vegetable selling in the covered market in Darlington. In time, four genera-

tions of his family were to become involved in his business, which functioned from the same premises from its beginning in 1884 right until 1971. It moved then, because of a huge increase in rent, into its own purpose-built premises in Oxford Street, where they still are today.

Jack Shepherd would travel up to London on a three day buying trip. Whatever was purchased one day would arrive home by train the next morning. Four horses and carts collected produce from the railway station and delivered it round the district. The horses were stabled in King Street.

Above: The premises in Market Place from which the company functioned from its inauguration in 1884 until 1971. (A stay of 87 years!).
Right: A picture taken on a bright, sunny day towards the end of October in 1955. The original potato business is now subsidiary to dealing in frozen foods but selling in the market still continues and net bags of fresh vegetables are being unloaded from this Shepherd's vehicle.

Currently, twelve vehicles, a mixture of lorries and vans, are used to deliver within a thirty mile radius of Darlington and are based in Oxford Street

They were the main agents in the district for Smedleys and also handled a wide range of packs from Lovell, Wall & Company Ltd., Coldcrops, Donellys, Northern Dairies Ltd., Ron Turner Ltd. of Grimsby and Frigid Fruits Ltd. Apart from Darlington itself, whose retailers could be served within minutes of an order being placed, areas such as Stockton, Middlesborough and Richmond, and villages lying in between, were assured at all times of regular weekly deliveries. For the most part supplies were carried in insulated containers by the firm's general transport vehicles.

At this time, according to the managing director, Mr Maurice Baker, the principle demand for frozen food in this area was equally divided between retailers and the hotel and catering industry. Peas and fish were the most popular lines, the fish especially in the smaller villages, but there was fairly widespread interest in the general range.

It is interesting to note that in the north of England, especially in mining areas, frozen bilberries enjoyed an especial popularity. This was probably owing to a long standing tradition among miners

Above: Taken on the same day as the picture on the previous page, this photograph depicts the amount of heavy work that the business entailed.
Left: A Smedley's frozen food van from the 1950s. Shepherds were the main Darlington agents for for Smedleys.

store the same duty was performed by suspended Winget-Dole plates. In both cases there was a 3 horse power Prestcold condensing unit.

On 21st September 1971 the company moved to its new premises and expanded quite drastically by taking over A. Edwards & Son, Potato Merchants and Helmsley Produce of Spennymoor. Purchase of Harry Moses and J.J. Thompson, fruit and vegetable merchants in 1964 had been one of the factors that made the move necessary. Shepherds went on to buy Wareings of Finkle Street, Richmond in 1972 which was a retail outlet.

which decreed that all lunch parcels to be taken to the pits should ideally contain a bilberry pie.

Low temperature storage in the fifties took the form of two sectional cold rooms with capacities of 1,000 and 1,200 cubic feet respectively. In the first two stores, built in 1948 and extended a year later, cooling was effected by the direct expansion of methyl chloride through pipe coils; in the larger

*Above: Another Smedleys van dating from the same decade. **Below**: A trade display including a selection of sea-foods. In the 1950s the populations of the small villages in the area were for some reason the best customers for frozen fish dishes.*

Over 50 years of wall-to-wall experience

AE Burt & Company was established by Mr A.E. Burt and Mrs D. Burt in 1945. In the late 1800's, his father Mr W Burt had seven shops in Darlington. It was his boast that there was one for each child!

The general run of their customers were not in the top income bracket so the Burts offered an exchange service, allowing them to bring in very old items for less old pieces in better condition. Business was also bolstered by dealing in coal with a contract acquired for delivering to local hospitals. Unfortunately fate turned its hand and the death of Mr Burt from natural causes and those of most of his children through enemy action in the First World War meant that the shops eventually had to be sold.

A family survivor, Mr A.E. Burt moved to Scarborough where he became manager and projectionist in a cinema. After marrying in Scarborough, he brought his wife back to Darlington where they opened a shop in Gladstone Street. Being cautious people they kept the security of regular paid work. Mrs Burt ran the shop whilst her husband worked as an electrician at Dove Electrics in the town. When the shop was in a position to support the pair of them Mr Burt gave up his job and both partners worked at selling second hand furniture. Mrs Burt bought and sold whilst Mr Burt collected and delivered. When the first floor-coverings became available on the market to buy Mr Burt turned his hand to floor-laying and became one of the first

Above: Where the story started - the shop in Gladstone Street.
Below: The vehicle Burts used in the very early days. Mr Burt can just be seen driving it at age 14 before driving licences were required.

flooring fitters. Just when all was going very well a gas explosion in 1972 blew up a street opposite the Gladstone Street premises. The Burt's property suffered considerable damage. The windows were blown out and debris and glass pierced and damaged all the stock. Mr Burt and

other members of staff were injured, fortunately none of them seriously. The stock had to be cleared out and the shop completely refurbished. Although this was an opportunity to start again using all their valuable experience, it was a trouble they could well have done without.

Another serious set back occurred in September 1979 when an arson attack caused the shop to be burnt to the ground. No-one could have blamed the Burts if they developed a fire phobia. This time all the stock was lost and the shop had to be redesigned and rebuilt. Fortunately the shop next door had

been purchased as part of an expansion plan. This enabled trading to continue and plans for expansion were put on hold but certainly not forgotten.

In spite of all their undeserved problems, business grew and the company flourished. The fleet of white vans with the red logo became a familiar sight on Darlington's streets and so remains today. Burts prospered in Gladstone Street for 47 years, by which

Above: One of the vehicles used in the early sixties.
Below: Mr & Mrs Burt's first shop on the corner of Thornton Street revamped, pictured in the early 1970s.

largest carpet store. The shop in Gladstone Street is still family owned but rented out to tenants.

The followed a number of further moves. A shop in Northallerton was bought and prospered for many years until it became too small to accommodate all the custom. Another one in Newton Aycliffe was rented for a number of years but this too was affected by changing buying patterns. A large unit in Portrack Lane, Stockton seemed more suitable and was purchased. Unfortunately, after a long battle, planning permission was refused and the store had to close. An old bus station in Hartlepool was the next experiment. An original and courageous investment, this was bought and re-developed to a retail store. However despite various schemes to counter it, vandalism and thefts meant that

time business had expanded and require more space. The current premises in Valley Street were acquired, making 19,000 square feet available. The business moved there and became Darlington's

Above: Devastation in September 1979 when the shop was burnt to the ground in an arson attack.
Below: The shop purchased next door in Gladstone Street.

trading there had to be wound up.

Due to the successfulness of the company's redevelopment of retail units, it diversified into property development, on a larger scale including warehousing and office accommodation. The largest development was converting the old William Press building in Darlington of 55,000 square feet into 19 self contained offices.

Perhaps furnishing these focused the Burt family's attention on the floor coverings for which the company is well known. The first type they dealt in was bitumen-backed linoleums which can still be purchased today. These are now only a very small part of the vast selection of floor furnishing choices available. Wool and man made fibre carpets are now predominant, in an abundance of colours, designs and qualities

With over 500 carpets to choose from Burts have products to suit all pockets. Cord carpets come the cheapest whilst the most expensive in the range are Axminsters. The firm offers a complete service, second to none, including estimating, planning, delivery and professional fitting. It prides itself on offering a complete personal service and excellent after-care, so that their customers return again and again, some of them second and third generations of the same family. Many new customers have been personally advised to come to Burts by previous customers.

Burts cater for the whole perspective of customers from private individuals, retailers and commercial properties all within a thirty mile radius of Darlington. On occasions the firm has dealt with customers as far afield as London but transport costs

obviously mean that this happens rarely.

Burts consider their virtues as vendors come from being a family firm of three generations serving Darlington for more than fifty years, so that they have become totally familiar with Darlington's preferences and requirements. They are committed to staff training and are the first company in the North East to have a carpet fitter trained to NVQ Level 2. Since then five fitters have achieved that standard and three more are currently pursuing it.

Burts feel responsible for the comfort and contentment of their workforce. The fact that a good many staff and retail fitters have stayed with the company for more than thirty years suggests that they have fulfilled that responsibility.

The companies mission statement is 'to be recognised as the provider of the best quality customer care and service to the North East's retail and contract flooring sectors'.

There is an expansion programme currently in hand for further development, with a new site opening near MFI Homebase on Russell Street, Darlington where customers will receive the same professional service maintaining its tradition of customer satisfaction.

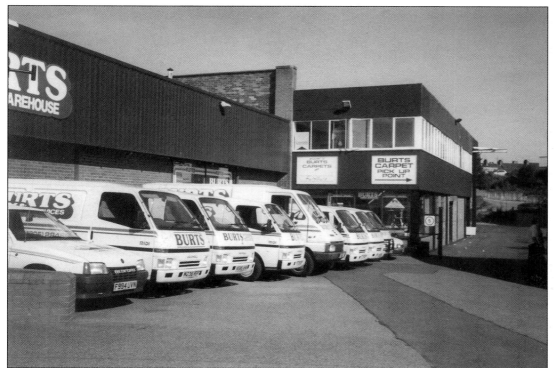

Above: Burts friendly sales staff are always here to help you.
Left: The fleet of white vans with their red logo, lined up outside the Valley Street premises ready for loading.

'Corner shop' to cornerstone of the local business community

This retail grocery business had humble beginnings. Ken Warne left school early and began working for The Maypole, making deliveries on his bike, patting butter and boning and rolling bacon. Seeking a position with greater prospects, he left to take up an apprenticeship at the Whessoe Engineering Works as a turner. It was during this period that he met his wife Vera whom he married when he was 21 and she was just 18. By then, war had broken out and aged 19 Ken had joined the Fleet Air Arm where he eventually reached the rank of First Lieutenant.

After the war he returned to Whessoe and, together with a friend named Cecil Attwood, attended a business course. At this time he and Vera were still living with Mrs Warne senior and her neighbour told the Warne family about a green-grocery shop that was for sale as a going concern.

After some persuasion, Ken's mother was talked into selling her house and lending the proceeds to Ken to buy this business. The whole family had to live above the shop and for Ken there came a period of very taxing work. During the day he ran the shop, whilst during the night he went to the Shildon Railway Works to give his new business some financial backing.

Trading had begun on August 4th 1948 and in its first week, the shop's takings amounted to £49 6s 1d. This sum was immediately ploughed back into the business.

Ken travelled by bicycle to the station on his way to his nightly work. He took the train to Shildon, having chained his bike to the railings from where he would collect it after his night's work.

Above: Ken Warne, founder of the company that still bears his name.
Below: Spar offers, a window poster assures customers, are available to anyone in any quantity. The window is full of them.

waste was considered a sin. Older sister, Carol was supportive too, helping in the shop when it was open and scrubbing and cleaning when it was closed.

In the very early fifties the shop next door came up for sale. It was acting as a sub-post-office and Ken was interviewed for the position of sub-post-master. When he was given the job he bought the next-door shop. By now, on doctor's orders, Ken had given up his night job. When the post office became incorporated, Ropner's Shipping Company would send money orders to pay the seamen and Vera spent hours writing them out. Gradually the business prospered and Ken began to reap his reward for the tremendous effort he had put in during his early life. 1953 brought success in a window display competition. Barry and his wife gave useful help in the shop and Ken's reputation grew as he learned his business and cultivated a professional approach to it. He joined the local Grocers' Association and was the first grocer in the region to join Spar in the late fifties. Some time afterwards he was elected a director of the Spar Guild of Grocers.

The shop was altered to cope. A whole new section was built to the rear and the rest of the building and the shop front were modernised. The outside of the shop had the largest Spar sign in the north of England, twelve feet long. Not one hour's trade was lost throughout the whole of the refurbishment.

before going to the fruit and vegetable market on Darlington Market Place to pick up supplies for the shop. His bike was very precious at this time. Without it Ken would have gone out of business and lost his job at Shildon Railway Works.

Friends and family felt that Ken had been unwise to take on so much responsibility but they had underestimated both his determination and his physical strength. After four years, the business diversified into groceries. His son, Barry can still remember the smell of the produce, especially the fruit, whenever he walked through the door. The family also remembers from this time a customer whose dachshund used to steal and eat raw potatoes.

Next Ken borrowed the money to buy an Austin7 van which he used to deliver orders within a ten mile radius. Wednesday was half day closing so that was the time that orders were packed up and loaded for Thursday and Friday deliveries. For five years Vera worked alongside her husband and Barry remembers his grandmother, Ken's mother Jane-Ann boiling beetroot on Thursdays in the shop kitchen where

Ken Warne STORES

LURPAK BUTTER	per lb.	3/6
2lb. SUGAR	only	1/1

when you buy a packet of Ten BIRDS EYE 'Regulation' FISH FINGERS for 3/2.

FRAY BENTOS CORNED BEEF		
7 oz. 2/10	12 oz.	4/3
DEL MONTE SLICED PEACHES		
A1 tall 1/10	A2 tall	2/11
ANDREX TOILET ROLLS		1/8
HEINZ SALAD CREAM	10 oz.	1/10
BLUE BAND MARGARINE	1lb.	2/8
KELLOGG'S CORNFLAKES	12 oz.	1/8
SPILLERS FLOUR Plain or S.R.		1/9
Large FAIRY LIQUID	only	1/7

WHEN YOU USE THIS COUPON. (Limited Quantity Only).

FD.11 5ᵈ

COUPON WORTH when you buy FAIRY LIQUID from branches of KEN WARNE 5ᴰ

FD11 5ᵈ

SPAR FOODLINER MOWDEN PARK
17/19 CLEVELAND TERRACE
WARNE & SEDGWICK 206 HAUGHTON RD

Above: An advertisement from the very early seventies just before the British currency changes.
Top: Ken Warne as a young man chats to Lady Isobel Barnett.
Left: The original shop after groceries had been included in the stock.

Barry had begun his career as an accountant. In 1970 he brought this very valuable experience to the family business when he officially joined it. Soon afterwards Ken bought the Mowden Park shop, going on to own seven stores in and around Darlington.

In spite of his demanding and varied working life, Ken has found time to be first (and last) a supporter of Darlington Football Club, then a financial director and finally in 1982 Chairman of the club. During a time of financial difficulty at the club, Ken had the idea of inviting Bobby Charlton to visit as a fundraiser. Also,

Above: The present premises pictured in the 1960s.
Left: Kevin Keegan and Ken Warne share a drink and a chat about the fortunes of Darlington Football Club.

Daughter Janice's degree was in business studies. She is a shareholder though she does not work for the firm, but son Terry joined it after gaining experience with a major multiple company. Now they are an independent company with a multi-million pound turnover. Ken and Barry are the first father and son to have been elected presidents of the Rotary Club of Darlington and to be elected presidents of the British Independent Grocerers' Association. The latter is now known as the Association of Convenience Stores, of which Barry was the founder chairman.

A recent policy in Ken's company is to purchase freehold all the properties from which they operate. This year the company was sad to have to send Barry as its representative to the funeral of Rose Johnson who had been Ken's very first employee.

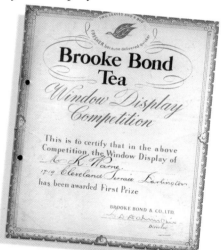

A long time before his own death in October 1984, Ken had made a particular request to his son Barry. If letters of sympathy were to be received from any of Ken's footballing friends or associates, Barry was to write a personal reply. In the event, condolences were received from the chairmen of every single league club. Barry was glad to acknowledge this great tribute to his father's popularity and command of respect.

Unfortunately Barry had to retire with health problems and the company is now run by his three brothers with Peter heading the team and their mother as Company Secretary. The Richmond shop is expanding and plans are being made to set up another outlet in another market town. The company celebrates its half centenary in 1998 and with the wealth of experience built up over this time, it can look forward to the next fifty years and beyond with confidence.

one of Ken's acquisitions for the club was the England Fullback, Cyril Knowles.

In 1976 Ken Warne Ltd was set up. It was a partnership between Ken, Vera and Barry.

Later more of Ken's children brought their various talents to the business. Kevin came in after completing a butchery course at Blackpool College and became a partner when a third shop was acquired. Peter, another son attended Keele University, reading Economics and German for his B. Sc (Hons) degree before becoming another member of the company. Older sister, Carol, in between raising her family, also worked with the company, combining duties in the Post office and the administrative office. She was also a key player in the installation of the company's first computer system in the early 1980s.

Top: Ken Warne greets Lord Peddy at a rotarian meeting.
Above: The certificate awarded to Ken Warne when he won first prize in a Brooke Bond Tea Window Display Competition.

Something sweet for Darlington palates

Murrays the Bakers have been part of Darlington life for over 70 years. There have been many changes since Jack and Nora Murray started their small bakery behind a shop at what was then 74, Durham Road.

In 1926 the road was renamed and older customers will remember the shop at 119, North Road, not far from the old railway workshops where Jack continued work as a joiner during the early days of the business. Jack's mother helped in the shop and bakery, particularly when baby Frank Murray was born at the end of 1923.

By 1939 the business had grown to such an extent that a larger and separate bakery was required. The Murrays moved to Maude Street from where they served the branch shops and a number of wholesale customers. After the war, Jack and Nora's sons, Frank and John, became fully involved in the business and it continued to expand under their leadership.

The first move outside Darlington came in 1964 with the acquisition of a business in Richmond. In 1968, Pigford's shop and bakery in

Cockerton was acquired, followed by Bestwicks' bakery on Haughton Green.

Jack Murray died suddenly from a heart attack in 1966, but further tragedy struck the family in the early 1970s. Son John was killed in a car accident returning from the Richmond shop and the next year the other son, Frank, died from cancer. The firm survived the crisis that inevitably followed, thanks to the loyalty of another relative and member of staff, Arthur Young. He took over the management on behalf of the directors until, after a brief spell in the oil industry, Frank's son John arrived to take charge.

Good Shopping!

MURRAY'S BREAD
Made by J.C. & N.H. MURRAY, Darlington

Above: An old advertisement placed in the northern Echo on June 6th 1944. The newspaper was reporting the D-Day Landings.
Top: The family and first staff outside the original shop. Baby Frank Murray can be seen in his mother's arms.
Right: The company's first van in the 1930s, purchased to service an increasing wholesale business.

Beginning in 1973, John's time in control covered another period of expansion. The bakery was re-equipped and more shops opened, including North Road(1974), Archers Northallerton (1979), and a unit in the Morrison Centre(1980) which was only a short distance from that first shop opened by John's grandparents. The company's first coffee shop was opened in Crown Street in 1983 and the first move to Cleveland, (a shop in Yarm High Street) was made just before Christmas in 1985.

Towards the end of 1988 the largest expenditure ever undertaken by the family firm was laid out for their move to a specially converted, modern bakery in Union Place, Darlington, incorporating the latest in oven and refrigeration technology. Shortly after this move, Murrays also moved their shop and bakery in Richmond into the thriving Market Place just in time for Christmas.

By far the biggest single expansion occurred in March 1993 when the business of G.T. & A. Guy was purchased with three shops and bakeries in Barnard Castle, Guisborough and Stokesley.

In the summer of 1994, Murrays were approached by Netto Foodstores to operate their first bakery franchise in the North East. The store was on Ormesby Road, Middlesborough and it opened in August 1994. A second Netto franchise was opened in May the following year in their new store in Darlington. This brought the company's retail outlets to 12 in number.

Many things have changed since those early days in Durham Road but one thing that has not been sacrificed is the well-known wholesome quality of Murrays' products. In fact, many of the recipes used today have remained unchanged and are prepared in the same traditional, time-honoured way.

Above: *The Northern Despatch in 1953 published this cartoon caricature of Jack Murray designing a new hot cross bun!*
Top: *The confectioners at work in the early 1970s. Even after 75 years very few operations are automatic and products are made with 'hands on' care.*
Left: *In 1976 Murrays were asked to provide a commemorative birthday cake for the renowned contemporary dance company, Ballet Rambert. Here it is being cut at a royal gala performance in the presence of many celebrated guests, including HRH the Princess Margaret.*

Taylors - the journeyman butcher who bought a whole street

Harry Taylor was a Yorkshireman, born in Sheffield, who travelled around the north of England as a butcher manager, setting up butchers' stalls and shops and moving on.

In 1922, seeing a niche for a business of his own in Darlington, he brought his family from Sheffield to Darlington and set a market stall there selling meat and pies.

His business prospered so that by 1922 he was able to purchase 43 and 44 Skinnergate and furnish the premises as a shop. During the Second World War, he supplied all the NAAFIS in the area. Business increased so that he needed and was able to buy numbers 41 and 42 Skinnergate and expand the scope of the shop.

BEEF & PORK BUTCHERS

TELEPHONE: 4716

H. Taylor & Sons

41-44 SKINNERGATE DARLINGTON

OUR SPECIALITIES
COOKED MEATS, SAUSAGE AND PIES...................19...

Above: A bill from the early days, just after the Second World War. It describes the business as Beef and Pork Butchers specialising in cooked meats, sausages and pies.
Below: The shop at 43 and 44 Skinnergate that later expanded to take in three more properties.

As Harry's sons grew up and left school, they learned the trade, so that when he retired his sons took over. Robert left the family business in 1952 to set up his own shop in Cockerton.

Sadly, another son, Cyril, died in 1957, whilst Dick left in 1959 to run his own shop in Hollyhurst Road. In the same year, number 45 Skinnergate was purchased to make the parent shop even bigger.

Jimmy continued to run the Skinnergate shop on his own with about 50 staff until he retired in 1975. He was proud to remember his purchase of the Smithfield champion of 1964 to butcher and sell.

After 1975 the business continued under his daughter Pamela and his nephew Tony. This latter partnership is still in operation with the assistance of Paul, Stuart and Nigel from the next generation of Taylors.

In recent years the company has developed and adapted to make the most of a shrinking market. Traditional butchery has been supplemented by prepared foods, pies and other convenience meat products and frozen foods. The delicatessen trade has been developed. In 1992 a factory unit was set up at Green Street for manufacturing the company's own prepared pies, sausages and other prepared foods.

"BETWEEN 1922 AND 1959 FIVE SHOPS IN SKINNERGATE WERE BOUGHT TO HOUSE THE EXPANDING BUSINESS."

Above: 'Sovereign' - the Royal Smithfield Show champion for 1964. It was a form of butchers' 'one-up-manship' to buy a prize animal, kill it and offer it as meat to their customers. This one looks as though it would have fed a good many at Mr Taylor's shop.

At work

The construction of the improved power station facility took place in 1939, the additional generators required 3 concrete cooling towers and two large chimneys. Darlington was rather slower than many other Corporations in organising its own electricity generating service. Public street lighting had been powered by electricity from March 1901. The supply of gas had been a different matter; the town was considered to be a leader in that particular field.

The nationalisation of the electricity supply industry occurred in 1948. Darlington's power station took on the role of a standby generator which was used at peak times until its final demise. The concrete structures in this picture were pulled down in 1978.

Above: The W.H. Smith's book stall on platform 1 at Bank Top station is seen here about to be modernised. The picture was taken in January 1973 and gives a good impression of the sturdy victorian arches and roof supports which have graced the station since 1887.

"DEVASTATION WAS CAUSED IN OCTOBER 1972 WHEN A GAS EXPLOSION DESTROYED SHOPS, A FLAT AND A HOUSE IN THE THORNTON ST. AREA"

Below: Devastation was caused in October 1972 when a gas explosion destroyed shops, a flat and a house in the Gladstone Street/Thornton Street area. Windows and cars were damaged in a quarter-mile radius but amazingly nobody was killed. The Northern Echo reported that shopkeeper Derek Raine, who was injured in the blast, remembered lighting a cigarette just before the explosion. A gas leak had been reported hours earlier and it was thought that passing heavy lorries had damaged the underground main, causing a build up of the highly explosive gas. Workmen and officials are seen here in the aftermath of the blast, about to make the damaged buildings safe.

This picture was first seen by readers of the Darlington and Stockton Times as far back as the 1940s. The group of around a dozen young men were in the place of last resort - the Darlington Labour Exchange in High Northgate. The building was pulled down many years ago but it had served

its role well on the site for around 60 years by that time. According to the posters it seems that there were just two messages the Labour Exchange staff felt compelled to get across to their visitors. There was to be definitely no smoking in the establishment - you could imagine any offender being boiled in oil

at the very thought of it - and the remaining posters extol the virtues of National Service. The late 1940s saw some dramatic changes to the struggling national economy; the coal mines were nationalised in 1947, followed by the railway and electricity industries in 1948. In 1949 the Pound was devalued by 30% and a series of Dockers strikes made certain that the last few years of the '40s would always be remembered for the gloomy economic conditions which characterised the first few years of peacetime.

Bussey and Armstrong - building a better Britain

At the end of the 19th century and into the 20th, Mr Henry Fell Pease, Liberal MP for the Cleveland Division, lived in a fine Victorian mansion named Brinkburn. The lodge for Brinkburn was in Woodland Road and the entire estate is now covered with modern housing. The house stood on ground which is now the yard occupied by Bussey & Armstrong, builders of Darlington.

Alfred Banting Armstrong and William Bussey were both working in the building trade when they decided to form a partnership in 1902 and set up their own building business Their first premises were at Hopetown, from where they began building the first houses in Trafalgar Terrace using imported timber and horse-drawn carts.

Help for the unemployed
In 1928 they were sufficiently well established to be able to purchase a 25 acre site at Cockerton from the Darlington Corporation. They planned to build a new garden suburb of 300 houses, ensuring work for 120 employees for the next three years.

The scheme was popular as it also provided additional employment in trades supplying materials. The site was near the then new chemical factory, bounded by Bates Avenue, West Auckland Road, the LNER Barnard Castle branch line and Stooperdale Avenue.

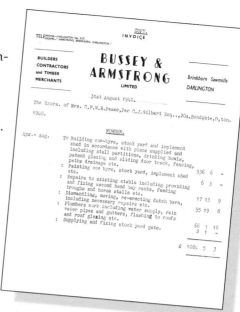

Mr A.B. Armstrong, then principal of the firm, was proud of using local materials. "There is no other trade that gets more of its materials from the local vicinity than ours. I estimate that the 800 houses will necessitate the use of over 5,000,000 bricks so that should mean steady work at the brickworks."

The garden suburb scheme had been devised primarily to provide accommodation when the chemical works opened. The houses, priced at £400, were thoroughly modern, semi-detached, each with three bedrooms, living room, kitchen and scullery, together with a garden plot. Even for the times, this was a bargain price but Mr Armstrong was concerned for his clients. "People cannot afford to pay big prices because their income has been so seriously curtailed. I will do my utmost to build these houses at £400 each."

In August 1940, after the death of Mrs Pease of Brinkburn, Bussey & Armstrong worked for her

Above: Dating from August, 1944 this invoice was for the redevelopment of a farm, including erecting a new barn (£55 19s 8d).
Below and facing page top right: *A sample of the post-war housing built by the company.*
Left: *An early solid- tyred tipper-truck used by the company for the delivery of sand and gravel.*

executors, doing almost £1100 worth of repairs to cow byres, sheds, stables, barns and gates. However, house building was the company's chief concern.

Early environmentalist

Mr Armstrong had a very responsible attitude to his customers and his town. An early advertising publication promises not only that the firm's houses will be as modern and comfortable as he can make them, but also that they will be 'designed so that every scheme enhances the beauty of the district.'

It is interesting to consider what exactly constituted 'every modern convenience' at this between-war period. Mr Armstrong was offering sunk switches in oxy-copper as the hardly-to-be-resisted feature.

> **"YOU DON'T RENT YOUR FURNITURE OR YOUR CAR SO WHY SHOULD YOU EXPECT SOMEONE TO LOAN YOU A HOUSE?"**

To call companies 'green' was not fashionable in the sixties, but work was held up then on the Mowden estate because a bird's nest full of eggs was found in a vital machine.

A whole section of Mr Armstrong's booklet is devoted to the purchasing of houses by ordinary people, an idea not taken for granted at the time. It points out, 'after all, you do not rent your furniture or your car; why should you expect someone to loan you a house?' Clear instructions are given on how to apply to a building society for a loan and how the society will expect to be repaid.

A 'new' garden city

Bussey & Armstrong wanted to bring to Darlington the 'garden city' atmosphere typified by Welwyn. The present view from the managing director's window, with grass-bordered pavements and rows of trees, proves that they managed it.

In 1950 the building of houses was suspended so that the workforce could concentrate on the new High School building. Mr Armstrong was pictured in the local paper overseeing the use of a mechanical navvy in the course of clearing the site.

A change in direction

In 1984, after the demise of both the original Mr Armstrong and his son, the present management under Mr Cooper took control. Because of the demand in Darlington in the eighties and nineties from the top end of the market, the company began to build properties in the £200,000-£300,000 price range.

These properties are traditional in design using real Welsh slate, brick and lead glazing. The company employs its own blacksmith to make finials and railings. The Woodland Estate is typical of the current style. It is a residential development in a walled parkland setting.

Whatever the price or style, this company has a reputation for housing Darlington people in houses that can be depended upon for convenience and value for money.

Above: An example of a new property built in a traditional style on the Woodlands estate in Darlington.

Above: A scene from the press room of the Northern Echo dating from the late 1950s or early 1960s. It is not clear just what was going in in this picture; the printers are gathered around the part of the press which folded and cut the sheets of newsprint as they converged at the heavily guarded whirring blades. Copies would come off the press too quickly to be handled like this when the machine was running normally, but would be taken by conveyor to the packing and despatch area from where they would be taken to the wholesalers and shops. The Northern Echo was founded in 1870, the first editor was the distinguished W.T. Stead. Newspaper editors are often keen to be remembered for doing things which are a bit different or unusual. Stead had the distinction of losing his life with 1500 other victims when the Titanic sank in 1912. A hard act to follow for successive *Echo* editors....but it hasn't always stopped them trying.

Masters of home knitting

Immediately after the Second World War, Patons & Baldwins needed to expand its production capacity in the UK. The firm would have liked to stay in its home area but most of the Yorkshire mills were not suitable for the latest machinery that had been developed that would have to be installed to make them competitive. They were also too scattered.

After discussion with the Government, Darlington was chosen as the site for major English production. Darlington was offering a level, 140-acre site and available labour. The move was made very quickly. Building began in February 1946. and by December 1947 the manufacturing of yarn had begun. Textile machinery had not had a high priority in war-time technology. Only one machine had reached a modest scale trials stage. The centrifugal spinner of Prince Smith and Stells ran at nearly twice the speeds of any machine before it. The Darlington development needed new machinery so its management took a gamble and invested in the new machines.

Above: John Paton, founder of John Paton, Son & Company Limited. Left: A penny pattern put out in the early 1900s. It features an easy, fancy stitch and uses Beehive double-knitting wool. Below: The Carding Shed at the Darlington mill which was 720 feet long and housed 44 carding machines. The picture dates from 1948.

Unfortunately the gamble did not come off and at the end of the 1950s these spinning machines had to be replaced by the new apron spinners. Meanwhile, by 1951, 34 acres had been covered with buildings. There was an office block with a magnificent foyer and a mill that consisted of a series of one-storey buildings that permitted the efficient flow of yarn through the various production processes.

Raw wool was conveyed by air suction to a nearby shed which housed 43 carding machines. The mill was air-conditioned and the power house could produce enough electricity to light a small town, being linked to the National Grid. Over six million kilograms of knitting yarn a year could be produced by the plant. The factory was also a major producer of hosiery yarn used by knitwear manufacturers. There was a canteen with seats for 1,800 people which doubled as a theatre, having a fully-equipped stage and dressing rooms. There were 50 acres of sports ground for staff including football and cricket pitches.

Both the Patons and Baldwins enterprises had acquired numerous firms since their individual foundation and this process continued after the firms' amalgamation. In 1908, J & J Baldwin and Partners Ltd. took over the Wakefield firm of R.H. Barker & Company Ltd., one of the directors of which was a Mr F.H. Wright.

In the grounds of the Barker millhouse at Thornes near Wakefield, his son, Philip Arton Wright was

*Top: Two ladies busily balling wool. **Above:** Kilncraigs Mill, Alloa. 1871.*

born in 1885. After training and service in the Great War, he succeeded his father in 1923, then became a director of Patons & Baldwins Limited. Technology advanced a great deal during the time of the Second World War and it became obvious that old-fashioned equipment in small mills was not the way forward if the company was to be competitive. Its work needed to be centralised.

When Philip Wright became vice-chairman in 1945 he was put in charge of setting up a modern Patons factory in Darlington.

He was popular with the workers who knew him well from his daily walk round all parts of the building, keeping careful note of what was

going on in each department and encouraging their efforts. He kept close contact too with many small dealers in wool, realising that, without the yarn dealers his company could not survive. He would personally greet small woolshop owners when they visited his factory. Philip Wright became the Company's chairman in 1951, and, when he retired eight years later, he had completed 56 years' service.

A portrait of him now hangs in the Boardroom. It was commissioned by his fellow-directors and painted by Sir Gerald Kelly RA as a tribute to the man who brought the company's English production facilities on to one site.

In the sixties the company experimented with retailing after acquiring a substantial interest in Fleming, Reid (Greenock) Ltd., with its chain of Scotch Wool Shops. After a number of years, however, these were disposed of so that Patons & Baldwins could concentrate on their more tradi-

tional activities. They continued to publish 'Stitchcraft' which had first been brought out in 1932. It continued as a monthly magazine with knitting patterns until June 1982. After that it came out every other month and consisted only of design collections.

During this period the company spun yarns from natural fibres such as mohair and angora as well as wool, and synthetic fibres, for example acrylic and nylon. The interesting designs they produced throughout the fifties and sixties helped to sustain the popularity of home knitting at a time when something more than economical basic designs was

required. From 1950, James Norbury, who can claim to be the greatest home knitting designer of the century, was employed by Patons & Baldwins.

Coats Patons Ltd

In 1961 there was a merger of two giants of the textile world. One, of course was Patons & Baldwins Ltd. The other was J & P Coats Ltd. Coats was a

Paisley company that exported much of the thread it produced in the 19th century to America. Coats merged in 1896 with Clarks, another thread manufacturer.

There were sound reasons for Coats and Patons and Baldwins to come together. The families who owned both firms had a great concern for the welfare and education of their employees and it was well to have this in common. Coats' needlecraft products were complementary to the products of Patons & Baldwins and both firms by now were selling on a world-wide basis. The new organisation operated 50 factories in 25 countries employing 40,000 people of

running a wool shop or yarn department.

A high profile with customers has been maintained through trade show displays, advertisements in women's magazines, fashion shows, competitions and charity events.

Further re-organisation became necessary in 1976 in order to remain competitive in a keen market. All manufacture of yarn for hosiery was transferred to other companies within the group and the factory at Darlington became the headquarters of the knitting yarn division and oversaw factories in Alloa, Greenock and Wakefield.

In 1980 it was decided that knitting yarn production should be concentrated in Alloa where investment was subsequently concentrated.

Coats Patons merged with Vantona Viyella in 1986 to become Coats Viyella plc, one of the world's largest textile groups. The Darlington site remains in use today as the warehousing and distribution centre for Coats Crafts UK - servicing retail customers across the country with a wide variety of products for needlecraft, sewing and, of course, hand-knitting yarns which bear the famous Patons brand.

Facing page, top left: A 1906 advertisement for Beehive wools.
Facing page, centre left: John Paton, Son & Company's selection of knitting yarns, offering wheeling, lambswool and super fingering.
Above left: The day's work over, the girls leave for home. This picture was taken before there were factory gates or gatehouse commissionaires at the Darlington factory.
Above: The main spinning shed in the Darlington mill which covered an area of thirteen acres.

many nationalities.

Since its earliest days the company has realised the futility of spinning yarn unless there is a ready market for it. They have ensured this not only through co-operation with retailers but also by educating them. In the seventies they introduced a training course for retailers covering such subjects as product knowledge, selling and various aspects of

Four generations on the rostrum

Thomas Watson was born in 1806 in London, the son of an auctioneer, and, after moving to the New Forest during his childhood, eventually came to Darlington in about 1832. First of all he is believed to have set up in business as a grocer. He possessed outstanding qualities not only as a businessman but also as a man of letters with a flair for poetry.

Having learned the art of auctioneering from his father he was ambitious to test his own skills in leased premises. In 1844 he organised a sale of woollen shawls and the flier to advertise it featured one of his own rhymes.

It was not until 1850 that the firm began its long association with Northumberland Street. Mr Watson was using his house in Grange Road as his business address but by 1851 he joined up with Thomas Bowman to form the firm of Bowman & Watson, Auctioneers and Appraisers of Northumberland Street. Though Bowman was younger than Watson his name was given more prominence. Thomas Watson had the flair and professional expertise. He had established good business relationships and trade directories

of the time describe him as a commercial agent and Sheriff's Officer, even, in 1847, as a paper merchant. However, his home in Grange Road was only rented and it seems likely that Bowman's part in the enterprise was to supply capital.

By 1850, Mr Watson was 44 years old. He had a wife, Emma and a son, Thomas William. His association with Mr Bowman lasted only 3 or 4 years and from 1854 he teamed up with a Mr Benson to form Watson & Benson. However, by 1860 Mr Watson was trading on his own again for a short time.

By this time Mr Watson was probably benefiting from the assistance of his son who would have been in his twenties and probably experienced on the rostrum. However, there is a public notice of an auction of 1863 showing the Watson & Bowman partnership trading once more from the Darlington Auction Hall in Northumberland Street.

By now Watson's name is first-mentioned. This second partnership ran for 13 years from 1865 to 1878. At the end of this period, Thomas Watson was 72 years old and would for some time have been letting his son, Thomas William, shoulder most of the responsibility. By 1879 directory entries read 'Thomas Watson & Son.' with, from 1885, the numbers 11 and 13 being added to the address. Today, number 11 is the saleroom and number 13 the Pet & Garden Shop.

Thomas Watson died at his home in Grange Road on September 13th 1883. His son Thomas William, now 41 years old was living in Langholme Crescent with his wife Alice and 4 year old son, William Elliot Watson.

Following his father's death, Thomas William ran Watsons, eventually training up his own son, William Elliot. The auction rooms at 11 Northumberland Street were jointly owned by

Left: This Victorian pram caused quite a stir when it was auctioned in the 1970s. It even achieved a write-up in the local newspaper.
Facing page, bottom left and centre: The contents of Woodside were auctioned by Thomas Watson in June 1915. The catalogue included pictures of many of the valuable lots on offer.
Facing page, top: Grange Road at the turn of the century. Grange Road was the home of the company for the first twenty years of its life.
Facing page, centre right: A very early advertisement for an auction held by Watson & Bowman in 1864.
Below: The Fred Robinson Showrooms. Fred Robinson is the present owner's grandfather who tendered for Watson's business after the death of William Elliot Watson.

Harry Robinson taking a Monday outdoor sale at Feethams Field in the early 1950s.

After his death the ownership of the firm passed to his widow, Ethel Maude Watson. Until 1950 the day to day running of the firm continued to be carried out by Owen.

In March 1950, after competitive interest resulting in offers made by tender, the business was sold to Fred Robinson and his two sons, Harry and Leonard.

The original name of Watson's was retained and Fine Art and Antique sales were held in the purpose-built saleroom. Harry and Leonard made structural alterations to form a large and spacious furniture showroom which became Saleroom 2. They eventually transferred the auction activities taking place at Feethams under the Fred Robinson flag to Northumberland Street, except for the outside sale every Monday.

two sisters, Hannah Soppet Rhodes and Ann Layfield.

Hannah sold her interest to Thomas William Watson in 1898 for £270 and Ann followed suit, selling her interest in 1907 for £200. The building which Thomas William now owned was in part that which is still in use today, although it had to be enlarged after a few years.

At this time, William Elliot was 31 years old, competent, dedicated to the business and very successful. When R. Benson and Son ceased auction activities from 13 Northumberland in 1933, William Elliot bought it and operated the very extensive premises formed by numbers 11 and 13 together.

Business during the first half of the twenties was prosperous but then came the Depression. From 1928 to 1940, William Elliot was assisted by his son R. Basil Watson. The latter summed up the situation during this period in a letter. "...prices were at rock bottom with £150-£200 being a sale total from a 10.30 am - 5.30 pm effort.' Whilst Basil was with the firm he was studying for his RICS and BSc and it is not surprising that he chose to follow a professional career in property valuation.

Owen D. Watson was William Elliot's younger son. He worked in the firm during the difficult years from 1940 to 1947 (with a break for war service from 1942 to 1945). Business steadily improved even though it was conducted against a background of labour shortage and bureaucratic controls which put all concerned under great strain, especially William Elliot who was no longer in the best of health. He died in January 1947, having seen the firm exceed the hopes of his father and his grandfather, the founder.

Harry's son, Peter Robinson was fully engaged in the business from 1971. He began at the bottom, driving the vans, then became saleroom porter. Only after that did he concentrate on saleroom procedures, fine art and antiques and the professional aspects of the business. Then he was thrown in at the deep end.

During an auction in Saleroom 2 he was summoned to the rostrum by his father to receive what he thought would be an errand. He found, however, that his father was announcing to the gathering that he had an errand himself and that his son would be

taking charge of the sale. He took up the challenge and has enjoyed selling ever since.

Today, Peter having already enjoyed 25 years of rostrum experience, is continuing the tradition by running Thomas Watson's from the original Gallery Saleroom. The fortnightly sales of Antiques and Quality Furnishings enjoy a keen following from both dealers and private buyers who are now furnishing older properties in their respective contemporary styles. The professional services, especially Valuations, are an expanding market and the firm's valuation department is now headed by Jamie Graham.

Thomas Watson's is keeping up with the future, check out their website on www.virgin.thomas.watson.

Above: Fred Robinson's in full flight with a fleet of Furniture Lorries.
Left: A 1970s open-air auction taken by Peter Robinson. Judging by the little boy climbing down the wall, everyone wanted to be in on it.

Seaton Leng & Son - caring for the local community

In the year 1891, Mr Seaton Leng founded a joinery and undertaking business in Gladstone Street, on the site of the old swimming baths, and settled his family into the adjoining house.

In 1920 the Leng family moved to a house in West Crescent, and relocated the business to its present site on the corner of Greenbank Road and Bondgate, where stables were erected with horse and carriage blocks. At that time the coffins were all made by hand from solid timbers. However, nowadays the majority are veneered.

Besides running his business, Seaton became a prominent figure in the civic and church life of the town, serving as Mayor of Darlington in 1920-1921 and later in 1927, becoming an Alderman. He was a Trustee of the old Greenbank Methodist Church where he had been a worshipping member for fifty years, ever since it had opened in 1879.

By the time Seaton Leng died in October 1942 his business had already been handled by the Bulmer family, and they continued to run it until the early 1950s.

In 1952, Mr Raymond Tindale joined Seaton Leng & Son. Mr Tindale who was also a member of the old Greenbank Chapel later became the firm's managing director. He was also appointed Northern Area President of the National Association of Funeral Directors.

Raymond Tindale's son, Peter, joined the firm in the early 1960s, learning all aspects of the trade from his father so that, on Raymond's retirement, Peter was able to succeed as managing director.

The 1970s saw a dramatic decline in the number of traditional village joinery and undertaking businesses. Today Seaton Leng & Son Ltd. are one of the largest privately owned Funeral Directors remaining in the North East of England, serving the needs of local families.

The funeral business is a twenty four hours a day, seven days a week commitment, and Seaton Leng & Son Ltd. maintain this traditional service. There have however been many changes within the firm since it was established. Not only have the stable blocks, horses and carriages disappeared, but also the old 1939 Rolls Royce hearse and limousines.

The modern fleet of vehicles is in a shade of burgundy, an alternative to the old fashioned black, yet still suitably dignified. From the nine private rest rooms to the fully-equipped hygienic preparation room and newly installed computer system, Seaton Leng & Son Ltd. have tastefully incorporated tradition with modern values.

Above: The 1939 fleet of Seaton Leng. Sadly this fleet is no longer in service.
Above right: Mr Peter Tindale, present managing director.
Right: The modern fleet which has been chosen in a shade of garnet to complement the quality service offered by the company.
Facing page, top left: Mr. Seaton Leng who founded his company in 1891 in Gladstone Street. Mr. Leng was a prominent figure in the civic and church life of the town, serving as Mayor of Darlington in 1920-1921.
Facing page, bottom left: Mr Raymond Tindale, father of the present managing director who joined the firm in 1952.

Bennetts - the business with a sharp edge on the competition

Rob Maxey is what the trade calls a 'saw doctor' and his 'practice' is the firm he set up with Ernest Bennett to manufacture and supply all types of industrial saw blades to customers in the North of England, Scotland and Ireland.

Formed in 1964 in Darlington it is a family firm and its story began in Sheffield when Mr Maxey and his uncle, the Mr Bennett of the firm's name looked for a new opening. They decided on Darlington because it offered such excellent access to the rest of the North East. Mr Maxey set up on his own in two small units in North Road, rented from Darlington Corporation, repairing saws, delivering and selling them himself. He decided to employ two apprentices at about this time, they are now the two company's managers. His office staff was supervised, as today, by his wife Iris.

In 1968 the Company moved to Middleton St. George. At that time the works produced wide band saws, between 18 and 30 feet long and between three and ten inches wide and were used to cut timber for house building, fencing products, the mining industries, joinery and furniture manufacturers. They also manufactured Tungsten Carbide Tipped Circular saws, precision ground for cutting from steel and timber to aluminium and plastics. These were circular saws with diameters from 100mm to 2 metres. The steel arrived in coils and plate form

Above: 'Saw-doctor' repairs saws, Mr Maxey inspects a wide-band saw.
Below: This illustration shows a typical example of the type of machines used in the factories in the 1960s for the servicing and manufacture of saws. This is a wide band sharpening machine.

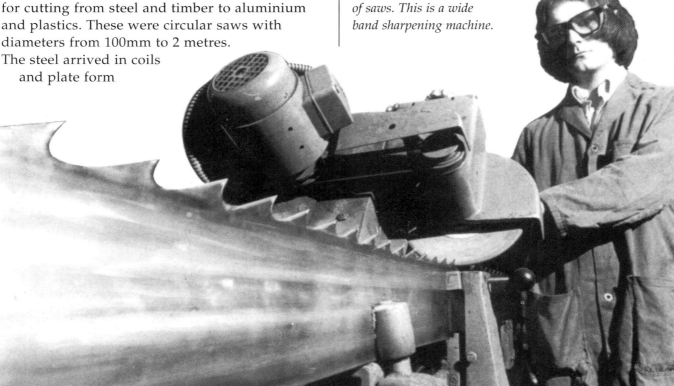

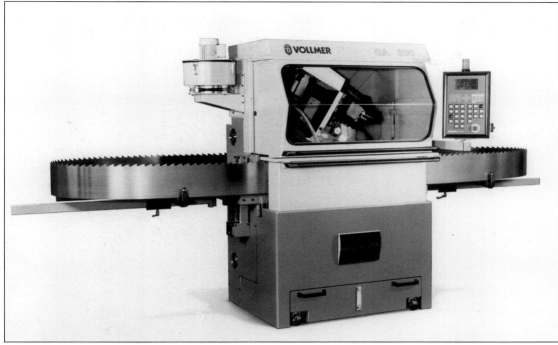

are surprised when they discover the full extent of Ernest Bennett operations which now includes a factory in Concord, USA. The company is always looking to improve its efficiency by introducing the latest high tech and high quality production systems.

and was then manufactured in Darlington. At that time about 70% of the firm's work was in doctoring their clients' saws. The life of a blade is unpredictable - a nail could wreck the teeth immediately. Every day vans left with new saws and returned with dull ones.

It was difficult in the 1960's to find skilled people in the area. All employees then, as now, were trained by the company.

As the labour market improved the company expanded steadily. It was one of the first saw blade manufacturers in the world to use CNC, wet grinding technology and CBN and Diamond grinding. It manufactured a wide range of saw blades and supplied customers in the plastics, metal, sawmill, joinery, furniture and timber industries.

Mr Maxey had decided early on that German/Vollmer machine tools were best for his requirements. The two factories in Darlington now have more than 70 machines and 55 employees.

The nature of a family business means that a more personal friendly service is offered, which may explain why many customers

Mr Maxey's son David, who is now joint Managing Director says, 'As our customers become more demanding in the performance they expect from saw blades, we are confident that with our substantial and impressive research and development programme, and our vast experience, we will continue to produce new and more sophisticated saw blades into the next century, giving all our employees job security.'

The company has a continuing expansion programme and is looking ahead with confidence to the next millennium. At the turn of the century (only two years hence) the company will have been trading in Darlington for thirty five years and is now one of Darlington's longest established companies still under original ownership.

Above: Mr Maxey decided that Vollmer machines were best suited to the work done by his company. This is a view of a CA200, one of the latest to be purchased. It is a CNC Computer Controlled Grinding machine for the automatic precision sharpening of band-saw blades.
Below: Ernest Bennett & Co. (Darlington) Ltd., Middleton St. George factory. Mr Maxey moved here with high hopes and the company is still expanding and looking forward to the millennium.

Cornmill - the evolution of a modern shopping centre

It all began in July 1984 when Pengap and their architect came to Darlington to discuss some ideas with planning officers. The first sketches they made showed a smaller scheme than what has now been built, but the basic concept was the same, a two-tier, covered shopping mall linking Tubwell Row with Northgate and across Priestgate via a large bridge. The biggest difference from the plan chosen is that the latter has a major link with Prebend Row. The fundamental idea accorded well with the newly published Central Area Local Plan.

Since the 1960s Darlington had slipped down the league table of shopping centres as competing towns carried out comprehensive retail development schemes and captured some of its trade. Darlington planned to follow the trend but controversial proposals involving the Market Place and Market Hall were rejected in the early 70s.

> **"ACCORDING TO RUMOUR A GHOSTLY APPARITION SUPERVISED THE BUILDING WORK."**

In late summer 1988 Burton Property Trust awarded Sir Robert McAlpine & Sons the main contract for the construction of the Darlington Cornmill.

Work was divided into two stages, the first being the demolition of the existing buildings on the site which began in September 1988. These included the large Co-operative store, several shops and offices and the Pied Piper public house, formerly known as the Raby Hotel. Demolition also included the clearing of large amounts of asbestos, a task which had to be completed with the assistance

of a specialist contractor. Several rooms of the adjacent King's Head Hotel were removed as well as parts of the Woolworth store.

All this was achieved on a carefully worked out programme that was designed to create as little disruption to local services as possible. The clearing of the 10,000 square metre site entailed the removal of 26,000 cubic metres of waste, mostly stone, concrete and rubble, before the second stage could be begun.

Building began in January 1989. One of the first tasks was to underpin adjacent buildings since it was discovered that these had no foundations. Settlement monitoring was also carried out. Other buildings were temporarily propped for support.

Above: A view of Tubwell Row looking up towards the Town Clock recorded in June 1988. This was shortly before demolition of the shops seen here began in September of that year.
Right: The arched entrance to the modern Cornmill Shopping centre is a well-known landmark to Darlington People.
Facing page: Prebend Row as it appeared in 1988 is featured in this photograph. Tubwell Row leads off to the right at the junction marked with J. Thompson's butchers. Further along Prebend Row, a mini-bus is about to set off to Red Hall.

Foundation work began with the construction of bored piles that would support the structure. This was done by drilling deep holes which were immediately filled with concrete. When the concrete set, the surrounding earth was removed, leaving proud standing pillars. This process was particularly difficult as much of the piling took place with the rigs hard up against old masonry.

The main construction has a re-inforced concrete frame. According to rumour a ghostly apparition supervised the building work as it proceeded. There are 876,000 bricks in the Cornmill which, if laid end

to end, would stretch 120 miles, the distance from Darlington to Liverpool. There are almost six acres of shopping on the finished site. The glazed scenic lift which gives access between floors and provides a spectacular feature in the atrium has a top which is almost 22 metres above floor level.

The APP Partnership, architects of the shopping centre are intensely proud of their achievement. Partner, Richard Hines, who took the original instructions in January 1985, has called the Cornmill the biggest challenge of his career and a flagship project for the practice.

Mr Hines was responsible for the original concept but he led a dedicated team within APP with particular contributions from a senior associate, Stephen Gray and project architect, Mike Doyle. The

> **"THERE ARE 876,000 BRICKS USED IN THE CORNMILL WHICH, IF PLACED END TO END, WOULD STRETCH THE DISTANCE BETWEEN DARLINGTON AND LIVERPOOL."**

team from APP found the Cornmill a technical challenge. It was built around many existing buildings. Also, the ground conditions posed many problems requiring decisions to be made on-site as construction proceeded. Importantly, the Cornmill has attracted new retailers to Darlington, unlike many shopping centres which have largely been filled by stores simply relocating within the town centre.

After their enjoyable visit to the Cornmill during

Above: An aerial view of the Cornmill Shopping centre which shows the blend between the tradition and the modern aspects of Darlington. In the foreground is St. Cuthberts Church, set in its own greenery with the shopping Centre behind with its distinctive domed roof.

personnel and other issues with ease and confidence. Every area is under almost daily discussion. His duties began well before trading commenced. In the shop fitting phase he held daily meetings with the clerk of works, fitters and clients. Regular inspections took place of all work in progress to ensure the high standards set by developer and architect were maintained.

The Cornmill files at the town hall run to well over 500,000 words - planning permissions, listed buildings and conservation area consents, compulsory purchase and road-closure orders, advertisement applications and so on. This is all besides the endeavours of all the engineers, building control officers and solicitors. The Cornmill workload adds up to a good many man hours!

construction, Skerne Park Junior School decided to compose a piece of music to celebrate its opening. The children concerned were asked to perform their song at the August 1992 opening ceremony of the Cornmill. Twenty children performed their song after holiday rehearsals to make sure they were note-perfect.

In 1994 the Cornmill was sold by Burton Property Trust to the Prudential Assurance Company Limited, who have continued to develop the scheme by expanding, in order to introduce new retailers to the town. In addition to this, the Cornmill has continued to re-inforce its community links, with its sponsorship of Darlington Civic Theatre's annual pantomime and links with various local charities.

The shopping centre is run by manager, Albion Small. His job requires a number of particular skills. He must be able to handle the accounts, marketing,

With the centre now into its fifth trading year, the Cornmill continues to confound its critics. The Cornmill has helped to completely revolutionise shopping in Darlington and is likely to do so for many years to come.

Top: The Grumbleweeds take time out from their roles in the pantomime to take part in a photo-shoot, promoting the sponsorship by the Cornmill of the annual panto. The sponsorship deal was successful in securing match funding from the National Heritage Arts Scheme, re-inforcing the commitment of the Centre to the local community.
Above and left: An attractive interior ensures that customers feel welcome. At Christmas it is bedecked with decorations which would fill the most sceptical of people with Christmas spirit.

Rexam - the firm that 'boxes' clever

The history of Rexam in Darlington has to begin with the history of its original raw materials. The story of corrugated paper dates from 1871 when an American, Albert L. Jones of New York, applied for a patent for a new and improved method of corrugating packaging paper. There is some previous record of paper being corrugated in England but no practical, large-scale use had been made of the idea.

The purpose of corrugating material is to give added surface strength. Fluted between two bronze gun barrels, the paper which Jones produced was made up by him into a primitive type of box.

Four years later the idea of sticking a flat sheet to one side of the corrugated paper was patented and this form of packaging is still used today. In 1881 the first power-driven corrugator was constructed with a unit for rewinding the board. A year later a patent was granted for a machine that could make both single face and also double backed corrugated board.

However, these developments were a long way from the giant modern machines of today. The development of the industry in America was limited by certain patent rights which did not apply in Europe and so factories sprang up in Germany, France and England.

The first use of corrugated cases for parcel post and the packing of bottles came in 1894-5. The invention at that time of the slotted folding box still used today set the seal on the production of a type of box which today continues to constitute 90% of production.

The introduction of the endless belt system carrying the board along the machine helped speed up progress and the manufacturing time of the board. With the increase of corrugated production, grew the need for better conversion plant. Printing machines were developed, at first adapted from printing wood together with slotting machines of various types.

Above: Samples of packaging supplied in the 1960s.
Below: Hugh Stevenson's premises from around the same time.

The First World War almost caused the death knell of the European industry but progress continued in America and percolated over to this country, so that the first European laboratory was opened in the thirties. In 1938 a new adhesive method using a starch suspension patent from America was adopted. Today it is the most widely used bonding agent in the industry.

The interchange of ideas and techniques has brought the industry together and led to the formation of the International Corrugated Federation.

The company Bowater began it's association with Darlington in 1966 when it purchased Hugh Stevenson & Sons who had established a corrugating plant on the Faverdale Industrial Estate in 1964. Since then it has been manufacturing corrugated fibreboard packaging and is now one of the leading designers, manufacturers and suppliers in Europe.

Above: Ready for the off! A works outing from the 1960s.
Top: A 1960s exhibition showing the process of box making from beginning to end.
Right: How things change! These packaging materials were produced in the 1970s and show well-known brands in long forgotten designs.

Yorkshire and to a lesser extent Scotland.

A few days before the official opening at Darlington the factory was open for inspection by relatives and friends of the staff. Two hundred invitations were issued and a display of the company's products were on hand for all to see. Guides conducting the parties around had difficulty in adhering to the timetable because of the extreme interest shown.

The tour took in all parts of the works and admiration was expressed for the surgery and other facilities created for

With satellite companies in Peterlee, Wetherby and a new factory to open in Leeds in 1998, it now has a combined workforce of around 370 and supplies some of the major manufacturers in the region including Flymo, Black & Decker, Samsung and Terrys of York.

Back in 1964 Hugh Stevenson & Sons held a sales conference in Harrogate and sent delegates to see the new factory at Faverdale in which the latest ultra-efficient equipment was being installed. The Piéce de Resistance was the corrugator, a machine 300 feet long which was, and still is today, the heart of any modern corrugating factory.

The timing of the opening proved to be ideal as it was able to relieve instantly some of the overburden of orders in the Errwood Park - Manchester and the Summerstown - London factories of Hugh Stevenson. The sales areas serviced from Darlington were Durham, Northumberland, Cumberland, Westmorland, East

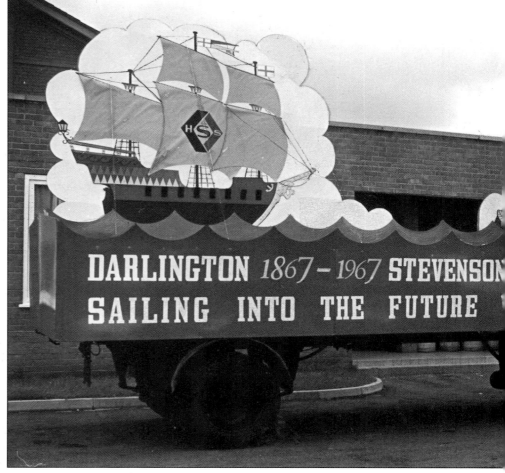

the welfare of the Darlington staff. With the exception of nine people, all the workforce had been recruited locally.

The whole of the opening ceremony was covered by both BBC and Tyne Tees Television and film of the factory appeared in both regional news programmes. Darlington newspaper headlines read 'Model £1 million factory hopes to employ 500 and 'Optimism at New Factory - 220 now, 500 forecast. The company flourished and fulfilled these expectations.

Above: In 1964 the Darlington branch opened, the ceremony performed by the Mayor and Mayoress. The interest was enormous, covered by both TV and radio and attended by hundreds of curious locals, many of whom were employed by the company over the following years.

As Bowater developed through the 1960s, 70s and 80s it became one of the U.K.'s largest industrial companies and had many businesses trading under different names including the corrugating plant at Darlington, which changed its name from Bowater Stevenson to Bowater Containers Ltd., and divisions in the United States which traded under the Rexham name. This was regarded as confusing to many of the large international customers and developed from being a minor problem in the early days to a serious

"OPTIMISM AT DARLINGTON FACTORY, 500 JOBS FORECAST FOR THE FUTURE."

From September of 1995 Rexam's distinctive blue and silver livery was seen on all company vehicles. The Managing Director, Mr. Trevor Bailey, pointed out, 'It is simply a name change. We will continue to carry on a successful business in Darlington .. progressing in the way we have for the past 30 years. Our name will be publicised much more widely and our smaller businesses will have the advantage of the major exposure of the Rexam name'.

The company celebrated its centenery in 1967 and produced this float, made entirely out of its own board for the occasion.

Over the last two years his confidence has been justified. The Faverdale plant has its own graphic arts studio and structural design centre where display packaging is quickly and cost effectively developed. As market leaders in graphically illustrated packaging, the company specialises in flexographic pre-print and high quality post print for the DIY, electronics, food, drink and consumer industries. A full range of printing options is available by using on-site and group resources for pre-print, screen print and litho print. In 1995, £2 million was invested in a state-of-the-art six colour post printing machine and a multi-point gluer making possible a vast range of packaging styles and in 1996 & 1997 a further £2m was invested in modern corrugating and diecutting machinery.

In addition to capital investment, the company is heavily committed to total quality and teambuilding and all employees are encouraged to participate in improvement activities.

Below: *The sheer scale of the Darlington premises is evident in this panoramic picture which probably dates from the late 1960s.*

commercial disadvantage, and so a decision was taken in 1995 to adopt a single name. The name Rexam PLC was chosen and following the usual world wide searches it was agreed this would substantially help the group attain it's objective of becoming an international supplier to customers who themselves had a world wide spread of businesses.

Subscribers

Presentation copies

Cllr. Mrs. H. K. Straiton, Mayor of Darlington
Andrew Smith, Editor, The Northern Echo
David Kelly, Managing Director, The Northern Echo

Mrs Ayton
Mrs K Campling
Alan & Edith Cook
Christine & George Cox
John Norman Davison
Mr & Mrs R Davison
Allan McDonough
Charity Olwyn Evans
David John Evans
John Dennis Fisher
Mrs EC Gattliss nee Botcherby
R Grover
Arthur G Harris
Norman F Harris
Daniel James Harsley
Mark Thomas Harsley
Mrs Horton
Peter King
Mr JM Lowery
George Kenneth Mason

Mr D McLaine
Mrs DW Metcalfe
Tom Middleton
Mr JE Newsome
Paul & Stephen Nicholson
Mr Pattison
Peter Ratcliffe
Mr Leslie Robertshaw
Andrew Robinson
John James Robinson
Derek Scrafton
Olive May Seaton
Peter Stephens
Vera & Alf Toase
Mary Thorpe
J Trathan
Paul Treslove
Mrs Chris Wade
Anna West
Maurice Wray

Acknowledgments

Thanks are due to the following people for helping to make this book possible: Andrew White and Peter Chapman of the Northern Echo, Kimberley Bennett and all the staff of Darlington Local Studies Library and Mrs Marjorie West.